The
DISCIPLINE
of
GRACE

GOD'S ROLE AND OUR ROLE
IN THE PURSUIT OF HOLINESS

A STUDY GUIDE BASED ON THE BOOK

JERRY BRIDGES
WITH DIETRICH GRUEN

NAVPRESS ◐
BRINGING TRUTH TO LIFE
NavPress Publishing Group
P.O. Box 35001, Colorado Springs, Colorado 80935

The Navigators is an international Christian organization. Jesus Christ gave His followers the Great Commission to go and make disciples (Matthew 28:19). The aim of The Navigators is to help fulfill that commission by multiplying laborers for Christ in every nation.

NavPress is the publishing ministry of The Navigators. NavPress publications are tools to help Christians grow. Although publications alone cannot make disciples or change lives, they can help believers learn biblical discipleship, and apply what they learn to their lives and ministries.

Printed in the United States of America

3 4 5 6 7 8 9 10 11 12 13 14 15 16 17 / 99 98 97 96

FOR A FREE CATALOG OF
NAVPRESS BOOKS & BIBLE STUDIES,
CALL 1-800-366-7788 (USA)
or 1-416-499-4615 (CANADA)

CONTENTS

How to Use This Guide

Shortly after my book *The Pursuit of Holiness* was published in 1978, I was invited to give a series of ten lectures on that subject at a church in our city. One night I titled my lecture "The Chapter I Wish I Had Written." The nature of that message was that the pursuit of holiness must be motivated by an ever-increasing understanding of the grace of God; else it can become oppressive and joyless.

The study and reflection that went into that lecture started me down the path of further study on the grace of God, culminating in a later book, *Transforming Grace*. As I sought to relate the biblical principle of living by grace to the equally biblical principle of personal discipline, I realized that it would be helpful to bring these two truths together in one book. That is the purpose of the book *The Discipline of Grace*. This guide is a companion to that book.

Each session contains an excerpt from the book and questions for personal study and group discussion. If you are working through this guide with a group, you will probably want to read the excerpt and work through the questions on your own before your group meets. However, if your group meets for ninety minutes or more, you could read the excerpt together and then discuss the questions that follow. This guide can also be used without a group for personal study.

Ideally, you should also obtain a copy of the book *The Discipline of Grace*, and read each chapter along with the appropriate study session. However, you can use and benefit from this guide without having read the book chapters.

In a study guide on personal growth in holiness, it should not be surprising that some questions ask you to reflect on the sin in your own life. If you are using this guide with a group, you may not feel comfortable sharing with the entire group your frankest possible answers to such questions. In such cases, try to be as honest as possible in the answers you write down for your eyes only, and share with the group only what is appropriate. You may decide there is one other person in the group with whom you would like to discuss some questions privately. In general, however, the questions in this guide are designed to be appropriate for group discussion.

Most sessions end with a suggestion for group prayer. In some cases, thanksgiving for God's grace is the fitting response to the discussion. In other cases, you will want to ask God for something specific. Since some groups have customary ways of praying together, while other groups are not used to praying aloud, you and your leader will want to adapt these prayer suggestions to suit your group. You could use them as a basis for a time of silent prayer if you prefer not to pray aloud. Or, you could begin learning to pray aloud by letting each person pray just one sentence. If you are using this guide without a group, you might apply these suggestions to a time of private prayer.

May God use this guide to help you grow in the discipline of His grace.

1

How Good
Is Good Enough?

*"Why do you call me good?" Jesus answered.
"No one is good—except God alone."*
MARK 10:18

CENTRAL IDEA

Contrary to a common misconception, we do not earn or
forfeit God's blessings in our daily lives based on our performance. Regardless of our performance we are always
dependent on God's grace, which is His undeserved favor
to those who deserve His wrath.

IDENTIFYING THE ISSUES

Excerpted and adapted from *The Discipline of Grace*, pages 11-27.

66 As I was sitting in the doctor's waiting room one day,
my eye was drawn to a remarkable picture of a man being
sculpted. The sculpture was complete down to about mid-
thigh, and the finished work showed a robust and muscu-
lar man with the kind of physique all men would like to
have. The striking thing about the picture, however, was
that the artist had put the hammer and chisel in the hands
of the man being sculpted.

I was fascinated by the picture and wondered what message the artist was trying to convey. Perhaps he was trying to paint a picture of the self-made man. As I studied the picture, however, I marveled at how it depicted so well the way many Christians try to live the Christian life. We try to change ourselves. We take what we think are the tools of spiritual transformation into our own hands and try to sculpt ourselves into robust Christlike specimens. But spiritual transformation is primarily the work of the Holy Spirit. He is the Master Sculptor.

The Holy Spirit's work in transforming us more and more into the likeness of Christ is called sanctification. Our involvement and cooperation with Him in His work are what I call the pursuit of holiness. That expression is taken from Hebrews 12:14—"Make every effort [literally: pursue] . . . to be holy; without holiness no one will see the Lord."

The pursuit of holiness requires sustained and vigorous effort. It allows for no indolence, no lethargy, no half-hearted commitment, and no laissez faire attitude toward even the smallest sins. In short, it demands the highest priority in the life of a Christian, because to be holy is to be like Christ—God's goal for every Christian.

Yet the pursuit of holiness must be anchored in the grace of God; otherwise it is doomed to failure. God's blessing does not depend on our performance.

Many of us believe if we've performed well and had a "good" day, we are in a position for God to bless us. This reveals an all-too-common misconception of the Christian life: the thinking that, although we are saved by grace, we earn or forfeit God's blessings in our daily lives by our performance.

So what should we do when we've had a "bad" day spiritually, when it seems we've done everything wrong and are feeling guilty? We must go back to the cross and see Jesus there bearing our sins in His own body (1 Peter 2:24). We must by faith appropriate for ourselves the blood of Christ that will cleanse our guilty consciences (see Hebrews 9:14).

God's grace through Christ is greater than our sin, even on our worst days. To experience that grace, however, we must lay hold of it by faith in Christ and His death on our behalf.

Regardless of our performance we are always dependent on God's grace, His undeserved favor to those who deserve His wrath. There are some days when we may be more acutely conscious of our sinfulness and hence more aware of our need of His grace, but there is never a day when we can stand before Him on our own two feet of performance, when we are worthy enough to deserve His blessing.

At the same time, the good news of the gospel is that God's grace is available on our worst days. That is true because Christ Jesus fully satisfied the claims of God's justice and fully paid the penalty of a broken law when He died on the cross in our place. Because of that the Apostle Paul could write, "He forgave us all our sins" (Colossians 2:13).

Does the fact that God has forgiven us all our sins mean that He no longer cares whether we obey or disobey? Not at all. The Scripture speaks of our grieving the Holy Spirit through our sins (Ephesians 4:30). And Paul prayed that we "may please [God] in every way" (Colossians 1:10). We grieve God and we please God. Clearly, He cares about our conduct and will discipline us when we refuse to repent of conscious sin. But God is no longer our Judge. Through Christ He is now our heavenly Father who disciplines us only out of love and only for our good.

If God's blessings were dependent on our performance, they would be meager indeed. Even our best works are shot through with sin—with varying degrees of impure motives and lots of imperfect performance. We are always, to some degree, looking out for ourselves, guarding our flanks, protecting our egos. It is because we do not realize the utter depravity of the principle of sin that remains in us and stains everything we do, that we entertain any notion of earning God's blessings through our obedience.

Your worst days are never so bad that you are beyond the *reach* of God's grace. And your best days are never so good that you are beyond the *need* of God's grace. Every day of our Christian experience should be a day of relating to God on the basis of His grace alone. We are not only saved by grace, but we also live by grace every day. This grace comes through Christ, "through whom we have gained access by faith into this grace in which we now *stand*" (Romans 5:2, emphasis added).

❖ Only a continuous reminder of the gospel of God's grace through Christ will keep us from falling into the good-day/bad-day thinking, wherein we think our daily relationship with God is based on how good we've been.

❖ Only the joy of hearing the gospel and being reminded that our sins are forgiven in Christ will keep the demands of discipleship from becoming drudgery.

❖ Only gratitude and love to God that come from knowing He no longer counts our sins against us (Romans 4:8) will provide the proper motive for responding to the claims of discipleship.

Without a continual reminder of the good news of the gospel, we can easily fall into one of two errors. The first is to focus on our external performance and become proud like the Pharisees. We may then begin to look down our spiritual noses at others who are not as disciplined, obedient, and committed as we are and in a very subtle way begin to feel spiritually superior to them.

The second error is the exact opposite of the first. It is the feeling of guilt. We have been exposed to the disciplines of the Christian life, to obedience, and to service, and in our hearts we have responded to those challenges. We haven't, however, been as successful as others around us appear to be. Or we find ourselves dealing with some of the sins of the heart such as anger, resentment, covetousness, and a judgmental attitude. Perhaps we struggle with impure thoughts or impatience, or a lack of faith and trust in God. Because we have put the gospel on the shelf as far as our own lives are concerned, we struggle with a sense of failure and guilt. We believe God is displeased with us, and we certainly wouldn't expect His blessing on our lives. After all, we don't deserve His favor.

Because we are focusing on our performance, we forget the meaning of grace: God's unmerited favor to those who deserve only His wrath. Pharisee-type believers unconsciously think they have earned God's blessing through their behavior. Guilt-laden believers are quite sure they have forfeited God's blessing through their lack of discipline or their disobedience. Both have forgotten the meaning of grace because they have moved away from the gospel and have slipped into a performance relationship with God.

We believers do need to be challenged to a life of committed discipleship, but that challenge needs to be based on the gospel, not on duty or guilt. Duty or guilt may motivate us for awhile, but only a sense of Christ's love for us will motivate us for a lifetime. If we are going to persevere as committed disciples of Jesus Christ over the course of our lives, we must always keep the gospel of God's forgiveness through Christ before us. We should, to use the words of my friend Jack Miller, preach the gospel to ourselves every day.**99**

DEVELOPING THE DISCIPLINE OF GRACE
   1. What's your initial reaction to this statement: "The pursuit of holiness must be anchored in the grace of God; otherwise it is doomed to failure"?

   ❏ The grace of God and the vigorous pursuit of holiness cannot be brought together; they seem like direct and unequivocal opposites to me, sort of like "jumbo shrimp."

11

❑ The pursuit of holiness sounds to me like legalism and manmade rules.

❑ An emphasis on grace seems to me like an open door to irresponsible, sinful behavior, setting us free to sin as we please.

❑ I realize grace and the personal discipline go hand in hand.

❑ I do not understand what it means to live by grace in my daily life, especially the relationship of grace to personal discipline.

❑ Other (describe it):

2. The picture of a well-chiseled man—with hammer and chisel in hand—depicts how many Christians try to live the Christian life. It seems we are always trying to change ourselves with self-help tools (hammer and chisel). Put yourself in that picture and consider this book as a tool available to sculpt you. What would be the difference between using this guide as a tool in your hands and letting God use it as a tool in His? What would each of these look like in practical terms?

3. Consider two radically different, but typical, days in your own life. The first one is a good day spiritually for you. The second day is just the opposite. Then answer the questions that follow.

My Typical "Good" Day	My Typical "Bad" Day
You get up promptly when your alarm goes off and have a refreshing and profitable quiet time as you read your Bible and pray. Your plans for the day generally fall into place, and you somehow sense the presence of God with you. To top it off, you unexpectedly have an opportunity to share the gospel with someone who is truly searching. As you talk with the person, you silently pray for the Holy Spirit to help you and to also work in your friend's heart.	You don't arise at the first ring of your alarm. Instead, you shut it off and go back to sleep. When you finally awaken, it's too late to have a quiet time. You hurriedly gulp down some breakfast and rush off to the day's activities. You feel guilty about oversleeping and missing your quiet time, and things just generally go wrong all day. You become more and more irritable as the day wears on, and you certainly don't sense God's presence in your life. That evening, however, you quite unexpectedly have an opportunity to share the gospel with someone who is really interested in receiving Christ as Savior.

a. Would you enter those two witnessing opportunities with different degrees of confidence? (Would you be less confident on the bad day than on the good day? Would you find it difficult to believe that God would bless you and use you in the midst of a rather bad spiritual day?) Why?

b. Think back to your last really "good" or really "bad" day. Did God's blessing seem any more *real* or *remote* to you on one day than the other? Why?

13

4. The question of good days and God's blessing raises the question of whether it is possible to somehow be good enough for God. How good would "good enough" have to be to please God? (What answers would Jesus or Paul provide? Have each group member look up one or more of the following Scripture texts and report his or her findings to the group.)

Matthew 5:48

Matthew 22:36-39

Luke 18:9-14

Luke 18:18-25

Romans 3:9-20

Philippians 3:4-10

5. Draw a simple timeline of your life, with three points of time demarcated: your birth, the day of your salvation, and the anticipated day of your death. Regardless of your age when you trusted Christ, the cross divides your whole life into two periods: you as an unbeliever

and you as a believer. When along this timeline was grace more than a theological concept to you?

6. Bridges makes the point that we have relegated the gospel to the unbeliever and foisted the duties of spiritual disciplines, holiness, and service onto the believer. Is that true in your own experience? Why do you suppose that happens?

7. The Pharisee-type believer and the guilt-laden believer both misunderstand the meaning of grace. How so?

8. How does "preaching the gospel to yourself every day" relate to this performance trap?

9. One practical way of "preaching the gospel to yourself" is to adjust the lens through which you read Scripture. With a corrective lens, you could see gospel and grace everywhere in Scripture and thus feel motivated. Without that lens, you might see only law and duty and thus feel unmotivated.

Consider, for example, what motivated Paul. How do you read 2 Corinthians 5:14? Do you think it was *Paul's love for Christ* that compelled him to do good works and pursue holiness? Or was the compelling factor, rather, *Christ's love for him*? (Read 2 Corinthians 5:14

in context and in several translations. You might also look at Romans 5:5 and Philippians 3:10.)

10. Mutua Mahiaini, the leader of The Navigators ministry in Kenya, Africa, makes this observation:

✦ ✦ ✦

God's Grace is GREATER THAN ALL OUR SINS. Repentance is one of the Christian's highest privileges. A repentant Christian focuses on God's mercy and God's grace. Any moment in our lives when we bask in God's mercy and grace is our highest moment—higher than when we feel snug in our decent performance and cannot think of anything we need to confess. That is potentially a glorious moment. For we could at that moment accept God's abundant Mercy and Grace and go forth with nothing to boast of except Christ Himself; otherwise we struggle with our shame, focusing on that as well as our track record. We fail because we have shifted our attention from Grace and Mercy. One who draws on God's Mercy and Grace is quick to repent, but also slow to sin.

✦ ✦ ✦

Are you willing to "bask in God's mercy and grace" as your "highest moment—higher than when you feel snug in your decent performance and cannot think of anything to confess"? How would you go about adopting this attitude?

11. (*Optional*) To some, an overemphasis on the gospel raises the specter of "cheap grace." Does knowing that your sins are and will be forgiven anyway permit you to keep on sinning and grow slack in your spiritual disciplines? Or does knowing forgiveness compel you to pursue holiness with all the more diligence? Compare your answer with those of Jesus and Paul, provided in the following Scriptures. (You could have each group member look up one text and report to the group.)

Matthew 23:23-28

Luke 9:23-25

Romans 6:1-2,15-18

Galatians 6:13,16-18

Philippians 3:12-14

Hebrews 12:14

12. Take a moment at the end of your group meeting to thank God for His abundant grace.

WHAT'S THE POINT OF ALL THIS?
The good news of the gospel is that God's grace is available on our worst days. Your worst days are never so bad that you are beyond the *reach* of God's grace. And your best days are never so good that you are beyond the *need* of God's grace. We will be exploring more of what that means as we look at the Parable of the Pharisee and the Tax Collector. Meditate on Luke 18:11-12 and read chapter 2 of *The Discipline of Grace* for next session. In preparation for that session, reflect on what it means to be smug and self-satisfied in your Christian life.

2

THE PHARISEE AND THE TAX COLLECTOR

"The Pharisee stood up and prayed about himself:
'God, I thank you that I am not like other men—robbers,
evildoers, adulterers—or even like this tax collector.
I fast twice a week and give a tenth of all I get.'"
LUKE 18:11-12

CENTRAL IDEA

We have points in common with both the Pharisee and the tax collector, the prodigal son and the older brother.

IDENTIFYING THE ISSUES

Excerpted and adapted from *The Discipline of Grace*, pages 29-43.

❝Christians tend toward one of two opposite attitudes. The first is a relentless sense of guilt due to unmet expectations in living the Christian life. People characterized by this mode of thinking frequently dwell on their besetting sins or their failure to witness to their neighbors or to live up to numerous other challenges of the Christian life.

The other attitude is one of varying degrees of self-satisfaction with one's Christian life. We can drift into this attitude because we are convinced we believe the right doctrines, we read the right Christian books, we practice the right disciplines of a committed Christian life, or we are actively involved in some aspect of Christian ministry and are not just "pew sitters" in the church.

Perhaps we have become self-righteous about our Christian lives because we look at society around us and see flagrant immorality, pervasive dishonesty, wholesale greed, and increasing violence. We see growing acceptance of abortion as a "right" and homosexuality as an acceptable alternate lifestyle. Because we are not guilty of these more gross forms of sin, we can begin to feel rather good about our Christian lives.

When we think in this manner we are in danger of becoming like the Pharisee in Luke 18:9-14. Jesus told the Parable of the Pharisee and the Tax Collector to those who were confident of their own righteousness, that is, to those who felt good about their own performance. As long as we compare ourselves with society around us and with other believers who are not as committed as we are, we also are apt to become confident of our own righteousness—not a righteousness unto salvation, but at least a righteousness that will make God pleased with our performance. The sin of the Pharisee, then, can become the sin of the most orthodox and committed Christian.

Most often our sin problem is in the area I call "refined" sins. These are the sins of nice people, sins that we can regularly commit and still retain our positions as elders, deacons, Sunday school teachers, Bible study leaders, and yes, even full-time Christian workers.

Refined sins include the tendency to judge others and to speak critically of them to other people, gossip, and unwholesome speech, even if what we say is true. We are simply not to say anything about someone else that we wouldn't want to eventually reach that person's ear. Only honest criticism given from a heart of love in a spirit of humility can qualify as that which builds up the other person.

Which of us does not offend frequently with our tongue? The real problem, however, is not our tongues but our hearts. Jesus said, "For out of the overflow of the heart the mouth speaks" (Matthew 12:34). So it would not be sufficient to win control over our tongues, even if we could. We must recognize the sin in our hearts.

Other refined sins include resentment, bitterness, an unforgiving spirit, impatience, and irritability. God is grieved over our refined sins just as He is grieved over sexual immorality or dishonesty. I am not suggesting that being irritable at one's spouse is as serious as adultery. I am saying that being irritable at one's spouse is sin and that *all* sin grieves God and should grieve us.

We have become too comfortable with sin. Because we sin so frequently, we learn to coexist with it as long as it doesn't get too out of control or scandalous. We forget, or perhaps have never learned, how seriously God regards all sin.

Three passages of Scripture that have helped me see the seriousness of sin are Leviticus 16:21 (where sin=*rebellion*), 2 Samuel 12:9-12 (where sin=*despise* or treat with contempt), and 1 Kings 13:21 (where sin=*defy* or direct challenge to authority). It is not the seriousness of the sin as we view it but the infinite majesty and sovereignty of the God who gave the commands that makes our sin a despising of God and His Word. The seriousness of sin is not simply measured by its consequences, but by the authority of the One who gives the command.

As we continue to probe the sinfulness of our hearts, we come to self-centeredness; selfish ambition; the love of position, power, or praise; an independent spirit; and the tendency to manipulate events or other people for our own ends. Then there is indifference to the eternal or temporal welfare of those around us and, finally, the cancerous sin of materialism.

There are a score of other sins we could mention, sins of the mind and heart that no one else knows about except God. But we have not even mentioned our failures to exhibit the positive traits of Christian character such as love, gentleness, kindness, patience, and humility. We are not only to put off the traits of the old self, we are also to

20

put on the traits of the new self (see Ephesians 4:22-24).

I found twenty-seven positive character traits taught by the Lord Jesus and by His apostles, either by direct teaching or example. I was not surprised by the frequent references to love and the conclusion that love is undoubtedly the primary Christian character trait. But I was surprised by the almost forty references to humility, yet how little attention do most of us give to growing in humility. The opposite trait of humility, of course, is pride, and there is no pride like that of self-righteousness, feeling good about our own religious performance and looking down on others'.

The problem with self-righteousness is that it seems almost impossible to recognize in ourselves. We will own up to almost any other sin, but not the sin of self-righteousness. When we have this attitude, though, we deprive ourselves of the joy of living in the grace of God. You see, grace is only for sinners.

I am sometimes asked, "As Christians should we view ourselves as saints or sinners?" We should always view ourselves both in terms of what we are in Christ, that is, saints, and what we are in ourselves, namely, sinners. If we refuse to identify ourselves as sinners as well as saints, we risk the danger of deceiving ourselves about our sin and becoming like the self-righteous Pharisee. Our hearts are deceitful (Jeremiah 17:9), and we all have moral "blind spots." We have a difficult enough time seeing our sin without someone insisting that we no longer consider ourselves as "sinners."

DEVELOPING THE DISCIPLINE OF GRACE
William Carey, who went to India in 1793, is often called the father of modern missions. His vast labors for Christ included translation of all or parts of the Bible into more than forty languages and dialects. Carey's well-known missionary slogan was: "Expect great things from God; attempt great things for God." Yet the same man penned these words:

I am this day seventy years old, a monument of Divine mercy and goodness, though on a review of my life I find much, very much, for which I ought to be humbled in the dust; my direct and positive sins are innumerable, my negligence in the Lord's work has been great, I have not promoted his cause, nor sought his glory and honour as I ought, notwithstanding all this, I am spared till now, and am still retained in his Work, and I trust I am received into the divine favour through him.[1] 99

1. a. How could a man of such remarkable faith in God lament toward the end of his life his own sinfulness and shortcomings? (Why would Carey not rather reflect with gratitude and praise on what God had done through him?)

   b. Should Carey's attitude be an example for us to follow, or should we write it off as an unfortunate bit of introspection that comes with old age? (Was Carey's attitude due to an unhealthy, low self-esteem? Or did it reflect a healthy realism characteristic of a godly, mature Christian?)

   c. Do you find Carey's attitude difficult to maintain in your own life? Is it motivating? Why?

2. If ever there was a person who excelled in the disciplines of the Christian life, in obedience, and in sacrificial service, surely it was the Apostle Paul. Yet he

viewed himself in a manner similar to William Carey. Paul kept "down-grading" his self-concept in view of the seriousness of sin. As Paul grew over the years, to what did he compare himself? (How did he "rank" in each case?)

❖ About AD 55, 1 Corinthians 15:9

❖ About AD 57, Romans 7:18

❖ About AD 60, Ephesians 3:8

❖ About AD 63, 1 Timothy 1:15-16

3. Now consider the Parable of the Pharisee and the Tax Collector (Luke 18:9-14). The Pharisee was orthodox in his beliefs and very committed in his religious practices. He fasted twice a week (spiritual disciplines); he was not a robber, evildoer, or adulterer (obedience); and he gave a tenth of all his income (service). To use our good-day/bad-day terminology, he was living in a continuous good-day scenario, or so he thought.

a. What then was the one fatal flaw in the Pharisee's thinking?

b. By contrast to the Pharisee, how did the tax collector see himself and his sin? (And in relation to whom?)

c. Why did Jesus declare the tax collector righteous before God?

d. How does this parable speak to you?

4. Jesus also gave us the Parable of the Prodigal Son (Luke 15:11-32). The emphasis of that story is on the compassion and grace of the son's father. Jesus could have stopped there, but He proceeded to tell us about the jealousy and resentment of the older brother. How is that older brother like the Pharisee of Luke 18:9-14?

5. While love is the primary character trait befitting Christians, it is also the most difficult to practice with more than mere lip service. To put "shoe leather" to the concept of love, try viewing the great love chapter, 1 Corinthians 13, in terms of action steps. As you read over these action statements on the following page from verses 4 and 5, ask yourself how you are doing in your day-to-day practice of love. On a scale of 1 (not at all) to 5 (always), how often do you tend to take these measurable actions? Circle the appropriate response. (Is there any room for self-righteousness in the light of this practical standard of love?)

I am patient with you because I love you and want to forgive you.

1   2   3   4   5

I am kind to you because I love you and want to help you.

1   2   3   4   5

I do not envy your possessions or your gifts because I love you and want you to have the best.

1   2   3   4   5

I do not boast about my attainments because I love you and want to hear about yours.

1   2   3   4   5

I am not proud because I love you and want to esteem you before myself.

1   2   3   4   5

I am not rude because I love you and care about your feelings.

1   2   3   4   5

I am not self-seeking because I love you and want to meet your needs.

1   2   3   4   5

I am not easily angered by you because I love you and want to overlook your offenses.

1   2   3   4   5

I do not keep a record of your wrongs because I love you, and "love covers a multitude of sins."

1   2   3   4   5

6. Bridges found twenty-seven positive character traits taught in the New Testament (see Galatians 5:22-23; Ephesians 4:1-2,25-32; Colossians 3:12-17; 1 Timothy 6:6-11; James 3:17). The traits are:

❏ Compassion	❏ Godliness	❏ Patience
❏ Considerateness	❏ Goodness	❏ Peace
❏ Contentment	❏ Honesty	❏ Perseverance
❏ Faith	❏ Humility	❏ Purity
❏ Faithfulness	❏ Impartiality	❏ Righteousness
❏ Forbearance	❏ Joy	❏ Self-control
❏ Forgiving spirit	❏ Kindness	❏ Sincerity
❏ Generosity	❏ Love	❏ Submissiveness
❏ Gentleness	❏ Mercy	❏ Thankfulness

a. Get a friend who knows you well to help you mark those traits in which you've grown in the past year.

b. Mark two traits you believe God would like you to focus on for growth. (Ask God to show you which two traits you should mark.)

c. In your group, discuss how helpful this exercise was for you. What did you learn about yourself?

To the extent that we miss the mark in these positive Christian character traits, we are sinners in need of God's grace.

7. a. Bridges contends that Christians should view themselves as both saints and sinners. Why is that?

b. How do you tend to view yourself usually—as a saint, sinner, or both?

c. How are you viewing yourself after completing this study session?

d. What will you do with what you have learned in this session?

8. Let the group leader close in prayer, using the prayer of the tax collector in Luke 18 as a basis.

WHAT'S THE POINT OF ALL THIS?
The point is to help us identify with both the Pharisee and the tax collector, both the prodigal son and the older brother. Whereas no one wants to identify with the Pharisee or the older brother, we are more willing to identify with the tax collector and the prodigal son. But are we really willing to say, "God be merciful to me *the* sinner" or "I am no longer worthy to be called your son"? Are we willing to admit that even our righteous acts are no more than "filthy rags" in the sight of God (Isaiah 64:6)? If you can truthfully say yes to these questions, then you got the point of this chapter.

Having reckoned with the seriousness of our sin, we are in a better position to apply the gospel of grace to our lives every day. In the next chapter, we will be exploring more of what it means to "preach the gospel to yourself." Meditate on Romans 8:1 and read chapter 3 of *The Discipline of Grace* in preparation for the next session.

NOTE
1. Timothy George, *Faithful Witness—The Life and Mission of William Carey* (Birmingham, AL: New Hope, 1991), page 155.

3

PREACH THE GOSPEL
TO YOURSELF

Therefore, there is now no condemnation
for those who are in Christ Jesus.
ROMANS 8:1

CENTRAL IDEA
When you set yourself to seriously pursue holiness, you
will begin to realize what an awful sinner you are. And if
you are not firmly rooted in the gospel and have not
learned to preach it to yourself every day, you will soon
become discouraged and will slack off in your pursuit of
holiness.

IDENTIFYING THE ISSUES
Excerpted and adapted from *The Discipline of Grace*, pages 45-60.

❝The gospel is not only the most important message in all
of history; it is the only essential message in all of history.
Yet we allow thousands of professing Christians to live
their entire lives without clearly understanding it and
experiencing the joy of living by it.
     We tend to give an unbeliever just enough of the
gospel to get him or her to pray a prayer to receive Christ.

Then we immediately put the gospel on the shelf, so to speak, and go on to the duties of discipleship. As a result, Christians are not instructed in the gospel. And because they do not fully understand the riches and glory of the gospel, they cannot preach it to themselves or live by it in their daily lives.

The single passage in all of the Bible that most clearly and completely explains the gospel is Romans 3:19-26. As we look over this statement of the gospel, we can see seven truths that we need to clearly understand.

No One Is Declared Righteous Before God by Observing the Law (Verses 19-21)

The word *righteous* means exact and perfect conformity to the law of God, which includes all of the ethical commands scattered throughout the Bible. The standard of obedience required by the law is absolute perfection (Galatians 3:10, James 2:10). Only perfect obedience is acceptable to God. We can never through our own obedience attain a righteousness sufficient for salvation. However, as believers we often act as if we can live lives acceptable to God.

There Is a Righteousness from God That Is Apart from Law (Verse 21)

Since we cannot attain a sufficient righteousness on our own, God has provided it for us. This righteousness from God is none other than the perfect righteousness of Jesus Christ, who through His sinless life and His death in obedience to the Father's will perfectly fulfilled the law of God. The righteousness of Jesus Christ is as much a historical reality as is the fact of sin, and in the book of Romans they are set in contrast to one another; that is, Adam's sin over against Christ's righteousness (see Romans 5:12-19).

Our Lord Jesus Christ perfectly fulfilled the law of God, both in its requirements and in its penalty. He did what Adam failed to do—render perfect obedience to the law of God. Then by His death He completely paid the penalty of a broken law.

This Righteousness from God Is Received Through Faith in Jesus Christ (Verse 22)

Faith is the hand by which the righteousness of Christ is received. Faith itself has no merit; in fact, by its nature it is self-emptying. It involves our complete renunciation of any confidence in our own righteousness and a relying entirely on the perfect righteousness and death of Jesus Christ.

Jesus Himself is always to be the object of our faith. We sometimes say we are "saved by faith alone," meaning, apart from any works. That expression, however, can be somewhat misleading, as though faith itself has some virtue that God respects. It is more accurate to say we are saved by God's grace through faith. Faith, again, is merely the hand that receives the gift of God, and God through His Spirit even opens our hand to receive the gift.

This Righteousness Is Available to Everyone on the Same Basis, Since All Have Sinned and Fall Short of the Glory of God (Verses 22-23)

God's plan of salvation treats all people equally, since all are sinners. One person may be a relatively decent sinner and another may be a flagrant sinner, but both are sinners, and God's law admits of no degree of failure. If sixty is the passing grade on a college exam, it does not matter if you scored forty and I scored only twenty. We both failed to get a passing grade. There is no point in your boasting that your failing grade is superior to mine. The only thing that matters is that we both failed the exam.

This eliminates any room for comparison of ourselves with others who may appear more sinful—or at least less holy—than we are. So if we are to live by the gospel every day, all tendency to compare ourselves with other believers, not to mention unbelievers, must be put away. Rather, we must measure ourselves against God's perfect standard and daily confess that we have sinned and fallen short of the glory of God.

All Who Put Their Faith in Jesus Christ Are
Justified Freely by God's Grace (Verse 24)
To be justified is to be absolved from any charge of guilt
and to be declared absolutely righteous. We are not only
discharged from all liability to God's wrath because of our
guilt; we are personally accepted by God because of
Christ. God sees us legally as so connected with Christ
that what He did, we did. Christ stood in our place as our
representative, both in His sinless life and His sin-bearing
death (Galatians 2:20). To live by the gospel, then, means
that we firmly grasp the fact that Christ's life and death
are ours by virtue of our union with Him. What He did,
we did.

Justification is a completed work as far as God is concerned. The penalty has been paid and His justice has
been satisfied. But it must be received through faith and
continually renewed in our souls and applied to our consciences every day through faith. There are two "courts"
we must deal with: the court of God in Heaven and the
court of conscience in our souls. When we trust in Christ
for salvation, God's court is forever satisfied. Never again
will a charge of guilt be brought against us in Heaven.

This Justification Is "Through the Redemption
That Came by Christ Jesus" (Verse 24)
Although justification is a "free" (gratuitous) act of God
as far as we are concerned, it was in fact "purchased" by
Christ with His blood. Christ paid the ransom that
redeemed us from God's just and holy wrath.

In God's plan of justification, however, justice is not
violated by a gratuitous pardon of the convicted sinner.
Rather, justice has been satisfied; the penalty has been
fully paid by the Lord Jesus Christ. In a sense, to justify
is to declare that the claims of justice have been fully
met. Although our sins are real and inexcusable, never-
theless God's justice has already been satisfied through
the "satisfaction of Christ"—He has fully paid the
penalty.

God Presented Jesus as a "Sacrifice of Atonement,"
Which Avails Through "Faith in His Blood" (Verse 25)
The atonement assumes the wrath of God against sin and
our consequent liability to His holy and just wrath.
Propitiation in the context of salvation means that which
appeases the wrath of God against sin. So the Lord Jesus
Christ by His sacrifice on the cross appeased and turned
aside God's just and holy wrath, the wrath we should have
borne. When we are acutely conscious of our sin and think
that God's wrath must somehow be hanging over us, we
need to remember that God devised a way whereby His
wrath against sin might be fully executed apart from our
experiencing the force of that wrath.

This propitiation is appropriated by us as sinners
through faith in His blood. The blood (death) of Christ is to
be the object of our faith by which we appropriate His sacrificial atonement. When we are smarting under the conviction of sin, when we realize we've failed God one more
time, we must resort to the cleansing blood of Jesus.

Nothing else cleanses us—not sorrow for our sin, not
our repentance, not even probation. It is the blood of
Christ, shed once for all on Calvary two thousand years
ago but appropriated daily or even many times a day, that
cleanses our consciences and gives us a renewed sense of
peace with God. 99

DEVELOPING THE DISCIPLINE OF GRACE

1. Sometime during 1993, a survey was taken on the floor
   of a large Christian convention attended by several
   thousand people. One of the survey questions was,
   "What is the gospel?" Of the scores of people inter-
   viewed, only one gave an adequate answer.[1]

   a. If you had been one of those polled, what answer
      would you give? Write your answer here and com-
      pare notes with others in your group.

b. What similarities do you notice in each other's gospel presentation? What are the core elements?

2. More than eighty percent of the people questioned by Bridges in group settings around the country indicate they'd be more confident of God's blessing when they've had a "good" spiritual day. Believers who base their everyday relationship with God on a good-day performance are little different than unbelievers who think they will go to Heaven because they've been "good enough." In Romans 3:19-26, how does the Apostle Paul speak to this misperception, common to believer and unbeliever alike?

3. The word *faith* is a noun and has no verbal form in English. Instead the verb *believe* is used, as in Romans 3:22. What does it mean to believe *in* Jesus? (That is, what is it we are to believe, or put our faith in?)

4. Romans 3:19-26 is loaded with theological terms that demand further explanation if we are to use them in conversation with our non-Christian friends. Explain the following terms in your own words, as if you were talking to someone with no biblical background. That is, do not use Christian jargon or long theological propositions, but do use secular analogies, synonyms, or short conversational phrases.

Verse 19: the law (of God)

Verse 20: declared righteous

Verse 20: (conscious of) sin

Verse 21: the Law and the Prophets

Verse 21: righteousness from God

Verse 22: faith

Verse 23: glory of God

Verse 24: justified freely

Verse 24: grace

Verse 24: redemption

Verse 25: sacrifice of atonement

Verse 25: blood of Christ

Verse 26: justice of God

Verse 26: justification of the believer

5. There was a great outcry when the late President Nixon was pardoned because many felt, rightly or wrongly, that justice had been violated by the granting of his pardon. Likewise, some do not like the way God justifies undeserving sinners, especially those with eleventh-hour death-row or deathbed conversions.

a. How would you feel if God justified convicted serial murderers like Ted Bundy or Jeffrey Dahmer by grace through faith? Why would you feel that way?

b. How would you feel if they were pardoned by the state after sincerely repenting of their sin? Why?

c. What is the difference between "justification" (by God) and a mere "pardon" (by a president or governor)?

6. Consider Paul's bold statements in Romans 8:1,31,33 in light of a recent bad day or failure you may have experienced. Despite what Paul says is objectively true about our standing with God, occasionally our conscience tells us we are under condemnation. Because of our frequent failures before God, we do not feel God is for us but rather must surely be against us. How then do we bring the verdict of conscience into line with the verdict of Heaven (Romans 8:1,31,33)?

7. "The blood of Christ," in connection with our salvation, is a favorite expression of New Testament writers. It occurs about thirty times, not just in Romans 3. What does it mean to have faith in the blood?

Romans 3:25

1 Corinthians 11:25-26

Hebrews 9:1-27

8. What aspect(s) of the gospel do you need to become more familiar with? What do you need to preach to yourself every day?

9. What stood out to you as personally significant in this session?

10. (*Optional*) Here's a practical way to preach the gospel to yourself every day. Meditate and memorize one or more of the following gospel texts, all of which offer assurances of God's forgiveness. You may prefer to meditate and memorize the texts cited above, which you've already worked with (questions 6 and 7). If you are really ambitious, try memorizing Romans 3:19-26. As an aid to memorization, write out the full text, and/or draw simple pictures beside the verse. All these wonderful promises of forgiveness draw your attention to the atoning death of Christ, the basis for pursuing holiness.

Psalm 103:12

Isaiah 38:17

Isaiah 43:25

Isaiah 53:6

Micah 7:19

Galatians 3:13

Colossians 1:22

Colossians 2:13

11. Close in prayer by thanking God for what He did for you through Christ. Use Romans 3:19-26 as a basis. You could take some time for silent thanksgiving or let each group member give thanks for one thing he or she sees in this passage.

WHAT'S THE POINT OF ALL THIS?
We will consider a number of factors that go into the pursuit of holiness in future sessions. But no factor is more important than learning to preach the gospel to yourself every day. In the next session we explore more of what it means to be united with Christ in His death, which delivers us not only from the penalty of sin but also from the power of sin. Meditate on Romans 6:1-2 and read chapter 4 of *The Discipline of Grace* in preparation for the next session.

NOTE
1. Reported by R. C. Sproul in a message entitled "The Priority of Righteousness," given at Independent Presbyterian Church, Memphis, TN, September 18, 1993.

4

WE DIED TO SIN

What shall we say, then? Shall we go on sinning
so that grace may increase? By no means!
We died to sin; how can we live in it any longer?
ROMANS 6:1-2

CENTRAL IDEA
There is no such thing as salvation from sin's penalty without an accompanying deliverance from sin's dominion. This obviously does not mean we no longer sin, but that sin no longer *reigns* in our lives.

IDENTIFYING THE ISSUES
Excerpted and adapted from *The Discipline of Grace*, pages 61-76.

❝The death of Christ secured for us not only freedom from the penalty of sin, but also deliverance from the dominion of sin in our lives. I realize that statement may sound unbelievable to some who struggle with sinful habits, but it is true.

In Romans 6:1-14 we learn what God has done for us through Christ to enable us to deal with sin, even persistent sin, in our lives. The gospel is far more than "fire insurance" from eternal punishment in hell. Through

Christ's death on the cross, we are given the ability to live lives that are both pleasing to God and fulfilling for ourselves.

Paul says it is *impossible* for one who has received grace to remain content to wallow in sin because one who has received grace has *died to sin* (6:2). This death has already occurred in the past. It occurred even though the believer may not be aware of it. We died to sin through our *union with Christ*.

Our union with Christ has two different aspects, bringing about two different results. The first is called a representative union. The second is called a vital union.

Our Representative Union with Christ
The classic passage on the representative union of Christ and His people is Romans 5:12-21. Paul taught first that all human beings (except Jesus) sinned in Adam as their federal representative. As a result, all of us experience death, which is the consequence of sin. Because of Adam's representative capacity, his sin was as truly our sin as if it had been committed by each one of us.

This representative capacity is somewhat illustrated by the concept of power of attorney. A friend of mine wanted to refinance the mortgage on his house to take advantage of lower interest rates. When the date for the closing was finally set, he realized he and his wife would be out of the country. He asked if I would represent them at the closing, and I agreed, so he and his wife executed a power of attorney authorizing me to act on their behalf.

I went to the closing and, as my friends' legal representative, signed all kinds of papers. When I signed those documents it was just as if they had signed them. When I signed the promissory note to pay a certain amount each month, that act was as legally binding on them as if they had signed the note, because I was acting as their legal representative. In like manner, Adam was our legal representative in the garden, and when he sinned, his action was as binding on us as if we had sinned personally.

We may object that we did not appoint Adam as our representative in the garden. To do so is futile, however, for in our objection we are actually complaining against God. It should be enough for us to know that God, the Sovereign Creator of the universe and the One in whom we live, and move, and have our being, appointed him.

The really good news, however, and the main point Paul was driving home, is that just as Adam was our federal representative in his sin, so Jesus Christ was our federal representative in His sinless life and atoning death. Therefore, just as Adam's sin brought condemnation and death to all his race, so our Lord's act of righteousness brought justification and life to all His race, that is, all who trust in Him.

Because of this representative union between Christ and His people, all of our responsibilities before God rest upon Him, and all of His merit accrues to us. Jesus, as our representative, assumed all the obligations in which Adam failed, and He fulfilled them on our behalf.

Therefore when our consciences condemn us for our sins or our failures to fulfill the disciplines of the Christian life, we must go back to the fact that Jesus is our legal representative and that in that capacity He perfectly obeyed His Father. When He pleased the Father, we pleased the Father. Our entire confidence in our acceptance before God is based solely upon the fact that Jesus was our legal representative in His sinless life and obedient death.

To die to sin then means, first of all, to die to its legal or penal reign and, secondly, as a necessary result, to die to its dominion over us. Sin no longer has any legal right to rule us. When Jesus died, He died to the legal reign of sin. Through our representative union with Him in His death, we, too, died to the legal reign of sin. But since the legal reign and the practical dominion of sin in our lives are inseparable, we died not only to its legal reign but also to its corrupting dominion over us.

We indeed do sin and even our best deeds are stained with sin, but our attitude toward it is essentially different from that of an unbeliever. We succumb to temptations, but this is different from a settled disposition. Our sin is a burden that afflicts us rather than a pleasure that delights us.

Our Vital Union with Christ

Not only are we dead to sin, we are also alive to God in Christ Jesus (Romans 6:11). Not only does sin no longer reign in death over us, now grace reigns through righteousness (Romans 5:21). The vital union is a spiritually organic union of the believer with Jesus Christ. By organic I refer to a living union. Jesus illustrated this organic union when He gave us the vine- and-branches illustration in John 15:1-5. The branches are joined to the vine by an organic or living union as opposed to simply being attached to the vine in some dead, mechanical fashion. In the same way, believers are united to Christ in such a way that we "participate in the divine nature" (2 Peter 1:4). That is, just as the branches share in the life of the vine, so we share in the very life of Christ Himself. That is why being "in Christ" was so important to Paul. It was not just a theological concept to him. It was the very essence of his Christian life. It was much more than a close relationship such as two friends might have. It was his very life. Paul lived as a branch participating in the life of the vine. He lived every day as a person "in Christ."

Not only are we in Christ, He is also in us. Christ enters into our humanity through the indwelling of His Holy Spirit to renew us and to transform us more and more into His likeness. This presence of Christ within us to make us holy is another assurance that we as believers cannot continue in a life of sin or have a continued cavalier attitude toward sin.

"Why," we may ask, "if we died to the reign of sin, do we need to be exhorted in Romans 6:12 not to let sin reign in our bodies?" Paul is saying, "Live out in your lives the reality of the gospel. Take advantage of and put to use all the provisions of grace God has given you in Christ."

Romans 6:11 says, "In the same way, count yourselves

dead to sin but alive to God in Christ Jesus." This is an exhortation to *believe* something, not to *do* something.

During the long years of the Cold War between the United States and the Soviet Union, a Russian air force pilot flew his fighter plane from a base in Russia to an American air force base in Japan and asked for asylum. He was flown to the United States where he was duly debriefed, given a new identity, and set up as a bona fide resident of the United States. In due time he became an American citizen. No longer under the rule of an oppressive and totalitarian government, he was free to experience all of the advantages and resources of living in a free and prosperous country.

This former Russian pilot, however, was still the same person. He had the same personality, the same habits, and the same cultural patterns as he did before he flew out of Russia. But he did have a new identity and a new status. As a result, he could discard the mind-set of someone living under bondage. Furthermore, as a benefactor of our government's intelligence establishment, he was furnished all the resources needed to make a successful transition to an American citizen.

The Russian pilot's experience illustrates to some degree what happened to us when we died to sin and were made alive to God. In effect, this Russian pilot "died" to his old identity as a Russian citizen and was "made alive" in a new identity as an American citizen. As an American, all the resources of our government were at his disposal to become in *experiential reality* what he had become in *actual status*. But this could not have happened without first changing his legal status.

When we as believers died to sin, we died to a status wherein we were under bondage to the tyrannical reign of sin. At the same time we were granted citizenship in the Kingdom of God and, through our vital union with Jesus Christ, were furnished all the resources we need to become in fact what we have become in status. We have been given all we need to bring the imperative—"do not let sin reign in your mortal body"—into line with the indicative—"we died to sin." But this could not have happened without a change in our status. And it is through our legal union with Christ in His death and resurrection that our status has been forever changed.

We must count on this and believe it. We must by faith in God's Word lay hold on the fact that we have died to the reign of sin and are now alive to God, under His reign of grace. Unless we do this we will find ourselves seeking to pursue holiness by the strength of our own wills, not by the grace of God.**99**

DEVELOPING THE DISCIPLINE OF GRACE

1. What do you think of this statement: "The death of Christ secured for us not only freedom from the penalty of sin, but also deliverance from the dominion of sin"?

   ❑ That statement sounds unbelievable, compounding the situation for someone who is struggling with one or more sinful habits.

   ❑ I've begun to experience that freedom from sin's dominion in my own life.

   ❑ Such a message of free and total forgiveness through Christ will cause Christians to treat sin lightly.

   ❑ I wish such a statement were true in my own experience.

   ❑ I do not understand *how* God delivers from the power of sin, short of finally throwing Satan into the "lake of fire," which won't happen until the end-time events of Revelation 19-20.

   ❑ Hallelujah!—what a Savior we have who can do more than we could ever ask or think.

2. How would you explain in your own words what it means to say we have "died to sin"?

3. Adam was like a king who involved his nation in a war, whether his subjects wanted the war or not. Do you feel it was unfair of God to let Adam make choices on your behalf that have had such devastating consequences for you? Why do you feel that way?

4. Christ is like a liberator who has freed anyone oppressed by sin who wants to join His side. How do you feel about getting free from sin just by trusting in Christ?

5. a. How would you explain what it's like to be united with Christ in a living way, as a branch is united with a vine?

   b. Do you experience this branch-vine connection on a day-to-day basis? If so, describe that experience. If not, why do you suppose you don't?

6. The common objection arises: "If we died to sin's dominion, why do we still struggle with sins in our daily lives?" How do you account for this continuing struggle?

7. Bridges says a cavalier attitude toward sin indicates that the person is not a true believer, however much he or she professes to have trusted in Christ for salvation. Do you agree? Why, or why not?

8. a. We died to sin; it is an accomplished fact. But Paul still says, "Count yourselves dead to sin and alive to God." What does it mean, in practical terms, to count yourself dead to sin and alive to God?

   b. Give an example of a time when you have had to simply believe that sin no longer had a right to control you. (Perhaps you have never done this. Can you think of a current situation in which you need to believe this?)

9. Think about the Soviet pilot who gained a new identity as a citizen of a free country but had to learn how to live out that new identity. How has your experience of becoming a citizen of God's kingdom been similar?

10. Close in prayer by thanking God for your union with Christ that frees you from both the penalty and the dominion of sin.

WHAT'S THE POINT OF ALL THIS?
We have seen in Romans 6 that salvation includes both deliverance from the penalty of sin and freedom from the dominion of sin. We have seen that our legal union with Christ in His death and resurrection secures our vital union with Him by which we participate in His divine nature and receive the power to live the Christian life. We will begin to address the practical aspects of sanctification in the next chapter. Meditate on Titus 2:11-12 and read chapter 5 of *The Discipline of Grace* in preparation for the next session.

5

DISCIPLINED BY GRACE

*For the grace of God that brings salvation has appeared
to all men. It teaches us to say "No" to ungodliness
and worldly passions, and to live self-controlled,
upright and godly lives in this present age.*

TITUS 2:11-12

CENTRAL IDEA

The grace that brought salvation to you is the same grace
that teaches or disciplines you. But you must respond on
the basis of grace, not law. That is why you must "preach
the gospel to yourself every day."

IDENTIFYING THE ISSUES

Excerpted and adapted from *The Discipline of Grace*, pages 77-91.

❝The title of this session may seem to some people like
an oxymoron. Discipline, to them, suggests restraint and
legalism, rules and regulations, and a God who frowns on
anyone who has fun. Grace, on the other hand, seems to
mean freedom from any rules, spontaneous and unstruc-
tured living, and most of all, a God who loves us uncondi-
tionally regardless of our sinful behavior.

Such thinking reflects a misunderstanding of both
grace and discipline. The same grace that brings salvation

to us also disciplines us as believers. Such discipline includes all instruction, all reproof and correction, and all providentially directed hardships in our lives that are aimed at cultivating spiritual growth and godly character (Titus 2:11-12). And though in the physical realm children eventually reach adulthood and are no longer under the discipline of their parents, in the spiritual realm we remain under God's parental discipline as long as we live.

We are performance-oriented by nature. All too often a child's acceptance by his or her parents is based on the child's performance. We carry this type of thinking into our relationship with God. To counter this natural trend, all our effort to teach godly living and spiritual maturity to others must be grounded in grace. If we fail to teach that discipline is by grace, people will assume, as I did, that it is by performance.

Another truth we see in Titus 2:11-12 is that salvation and spiritual discipline are inseparable. The grace that brings salvation to us also disciplines us. God never saves people and leaves them alone to continue in their immaturity and sinful lifestyle. Those whom He saves, He disciplines.

This thought is both encouraging and sobering. It is encouraging because our spiritual growth is not left to our initiative, nor is it dependent upon our wisdom to know in which areas and in which direction we need to grow. Rather, God Himself initiates and superintends our spiritual growth. Not that we have no responsibility to respond to God's spiritual child-training in our lives—rather, God is the One in charge of our training.

This inseparability of God's grace and spiritual discipline is also a sobering truth. Multitudes of people claim to have trusted in Christ at some time but do not seem to have experienced any of the discipline of grace. They may have walked up an aisle, signed a card, or even prayed a prayer, but grace is not teaching them to say no to ungodliness and worldly passions, let alone to live self-controlled, upright, and godly lives. Essentially, their lives are no different today than they were before they professed to have trusted Christ.

Each of us should reflect upon this sobering truth. Is God's grace disciplining me? We do not pursue holiness or the evidences of God's discipline in order to attain salvation. That would be salvation by works. Rather, God's discipline in our lives and our desire to pursue holiness, be it ever so faint, are the inevitable results of receiving God's gift of salvation by faith. Martin Luther said, "We are saved by faith alone, but the faith that saves is never alone."

According to Titus 2:11-12, the discipline that grace administers to us has both a negative and a positive aspect. This should not surprise us when we think of discipline as child-training. Every responsible parent wants not only to deal with misbehavior in a child but also to promote positive character traits. Both are necessary in physical child-training, and both are necessary in the spiritual realm.

Grace first teaches us to say no to ungodliness and worldly passions (Romans 1:18-32). Ungodliness, however, in its broadest form basically comprises disregarding God, ignoring Him, or not taking Him into account in one's life. It is a lack of fear and reverence for Him.

When we trust in Christ as our Savior, we bring a *habit* of ungodliness into our Christian lives. Grace teaches us to renounce this attitude (as well as actions) of ungodliness. Obviously this training does not occur all at once. In fact, God will be rooting out ungodliness from our lives as long as we live on this earth.

Grace also teaches us to say no to worldly passions, the inordinate desire for and preoccupation with the things of this life, such as possessions, prestige, pleasure, or power. Worldly passion is the opposite of the attitude Paul urged on us when he wrote, "Those who use the things of the world, [should live] as if not engrossed in them. For this world in its present form is passing away" (1 Corinthians 7:31).

The Christian life, however, should also be directed toward the positive expressions of Christian character, what Paul called the fruit of the Spirit in Galatians 5:22. In fact, all of Paul's ethical teaching is characterized by this twofold approach of putting off the old self and putting on the new self (Ephesians 4:22-24).

This twofold approach of "putting off" and "putting on" is like the two blades of a pair of scissors. A single scissors blade is useless as far as doing the job for which it was designed. The two blades must be joined together at the pivot point and must work together to be effective. The scissors illustrates this spiritual principle: We must work simultaneously at putting off the characteristics of our old selves and putting on the characteristics of the new selves, as one without the other is not effective.

Positively expressed, the Christian life "[teaches us] to live self-controlled, upright and godly lives in this present age" (Titus 2:12). These three words—*self-controlled, upright,* and *godly*—most likely refer to actions with regard to one's self, one's neighbor, and God. Self-control expresses the self-restraint we need to practice toward the good and legitimate things of life, as well as the outright denial of things clearly sinful. Upright or righteous conduct refers to just and right actions toward other people, doing to them what we would have them do to us (Matthew 7:12). Godliness is having a regard for God's glory and God's will in every aspect of our lives, doing everything out of reverence and love for Him.

With all this emphasis on practical Christian living, however, we must not lose sight of the fact that it is grace—not law—that teaches us. When I first became a Christian I regarded the Bible largely as a rule book. My perception was that the Bible would tell me what to do (or not do), and I would simply obey. It was as easy as that, so I thought in my new Christian naiveté.

What does it mean that God administers His discipline in the realm of grace, not law? It means that all His teaching, training, and discipline are administered in love and for our spiritual welfare. God is never angry with us, though He is often grieved at our sins. So where the law condemns, grace forgives through the Lord Jesus Christ. Where the law commands but gives no power, grace commands but does give power through the Holy Spirit who lives and works within us. **99**

DEVELOPING THE DISCIPLINE OF GRACE

1. a. Bridges contends that his title, "Disciplined by Grace," seems like an oxymoron (like "cruel kindness") to those who feel discipline and grace are opposites. From your background, what connotations do you associate with *discipline*?

   b. What connotations do you associate with *grace*?

   c. Do these terms seem like opposites to you? Explain.

2. Bridges is now grateful for the grace-filled, foundational disciplines of the Christian life, especially daily quiet time, Bible study, Scripture memorization, and prayer. But when he first became a Christian, he regarded the Bible largely as a rule book telling what to do (or not do). The practical "shoulda-oughta-gotta" precepts of the Bible commanded, but they gave no ability to obey. They left him feeling both guilty and helpless—all because of recurring sin patterns that were resistant to more and more Bible study.

   a. What are some of the disciplines of the Christian life to which you were first exposed when you became a Christian?

b. Which of those disciplines are you still keeping up and why?

c. Which have fallen by the wayside and why?

d. How do you feel about that?

3. a. Are you like the student who explained that he was rigid in his practice of a daily quiet time "so nothing bad will happen to me"? Do you sense God's smile or frown depends on whether or not you do your spiritual exercises?

b. What is wrong with that kind of thinking?

c. How does one lay a proper foundation and motivation for spiritual growth?

4. Many of us have friends and relatives who profess to be Christians but in whose lives there appears to be no evidence of the discipline of grace. Oftentimes we cling to a frail hope that such persons are believers because they made a profession some time ago, but with nothing to show for it. It seems parents are especially prone to this form of denial regarding children who show no evidence of a genuine work of grace. Without making any judgments as to the reality of another person's salvation, what are you looking for as evidence that a friend or family member is indeed a Christian?

Note to the leader: It may be appropriate to take time for prayer in response to the group members' answers to question 4 before going on to the next question. Instead of clinging to what may well be a false hope, we should pray earnestly that God will bring such people to salvation, or if perchance He has, will begin to manifest the discipline of grace in the person's life.

5. What does it look like in practice to say no to ungodliness and worldly passions? For instance, consider a person who has such a strong passion to be applauded for achievements at work that he neglects his family. What would be involved in this person saying no to his worldly passion?

6. Take a minute on your own to think of any ungodliness or worldly passion to which you need to say no. Write it down.

7. In Ephesians 4:22-32, Paul stresses that putting off sinful habits and putting on Christlike ones deserve equal attention from us. For instance, in 4:28 he tells thieves not only to put off stealing, but also to put on generosity. If someone in our fellowship who had been stealing made a definitive break with that practice, we would rejoice over a major victory won. But Paul would not be satisfied until that person had also acquired a generous spirit of helping others in need.

   This brings to mind three attitudes we can have toward money and possessions. Which of these attitudes sounds most like the way you live your life?

   ❑ "What's yours is mine; I will take it."
   ❑ "What's mine is mine; I will keep it."
   ❑ "What's mine is God's; I will share it."

8. The principle of putting off/putting on is seen again in our speech (Ephesians 4:29). We are to put off unwholesome talk (not just vulgar speech or obscene jokes, but also criticism, complaining, gossip, and the like) and put on what is constructive, thankful, and builds up others. Which of these attitudes sounds most like you?

   ❑ "If I don't have anything nice to say, I don't say anything at all."
   ❑ "It's not enough to stop complaining; I will start being constructive."
   ❑ "My speech is always wholesome, edifying to others, and full of thanksgiving to God."
   ❑ Other (describe it):

9. Here is one final checklist to measure how you sense you are being disciplined. Check True (T) or False (F), whichever applies to you. Talk and pray with your group about any area that you need help with.

55

T F

❑ ❑ While God *is* disciplining me by His grace, I perceive it as more by law.

❑ ❑ I see the grace of God disciplining me, even by His Word and adverse circumstances.

❑ ❑ I labor under the burden of guilt.

❑ ❑ I accept the forgiveness of God's grace.

❑ ❑ The Bible is only a rule book of commands that I am struggling to obey by my own willpower.

❑ ❑ I am relying on my union with Christ and the indwelling Holy Spirit for the power to respond to God's training.

10. Close in prayer by thanking God for all that He has been teaching you by His grace.

WHAT'S THE POINT OF ALL THIS?

With all this emphasis on practical Christian living, we must not lose sight of the fact that it is grace—not law—that teaches us. In the next session, we will begin to address the agent of godliness, or the power of grace, to transform us into God's likeness. Meditate on 2 Corinthians 3:18 and read chapter 6 of *The Discipline of Grace* in preparation for the next session.

6

TRANSFORMED
INTO HIS LIKENESS

*But we all, with unveiled face beholding as in a mirror
the glory of the Lord, are being transformed
into the same image from glory to glory,
just as from the Lord, the Spirit.*

2 CORINTHIANS 3:18, NASB

CENTRAL IDEA
The Spirit of God transforms us. He calls on us to cooperate and to do the part He assigns us to do—to behold the glory of the Lord—but He is the One who works deep within our character to change us.

IDENTIFYING THE ISSUES
Excerpted and adapted from *The Discipline of Grace*, pages 93-109.

❝The same word that describes the transformation of a caterpillar into a butterfly describes the spiritual transformation in the life of a Christian. "Transformation" in 2 Corinthians 3:18 is *metamorphoomai* in Greek, the same word that gives us the term *metamorphosis*.

The process of transformation (or "sanctification") is the work of the Holy Spirit in us, whereby our inner being is progressively changed, freeing us more and more from sinful traits and developing within us over time the virtues of Christlike character.

Sanctification begins at our conversion, when by an act called regeneration, or the new birth, the principle of spiritual life is planted within us. In Ezekiel 36:26-27 God says, "I will give you a new heart and put a new spirit in you; I will remove from you your heart of stone and give you a heart of flesh. And I will put my Spirit in you and move you to follow my decrees and be careful to keep my laws."

Note the radical change described here. The heart of stone is transformed into a heart of flesh. Matthew Henry says, "Renewing grace works as great a change in the soul as the turning of a dead stone into living flesh."

Regeneration, then, is the beginning of sanctification or transformation. Sanctification is the carrying out of regeneration to its intended end.

The goal of sanctification is likeness to our Lord Jesus Christ. Paul said in 2 Corinthians 3:18 that we "are being transformed into his likeness." In Romans 8:29 he said that God "predestined [all believers] to be conformed to the likeness of his Son." Both words, *transformed* and *conformed*, have a common root, *form*, meaning a pattern or a mold. "Being transformed" refers to the process; "conformed" refers to the finished product. Jesus is our pattern or mold. We are being transformed so that we will eventually be conformed to the likeness of Jesus.

We can easily see from the pattern of Jesus' life that conformity to Him is a lifelong process. That is why Paul refers to the continual change being wrought in us with his expression, "with ever-increasing glory," or "from glory to glory" (NASB).

Because sanctification is a process, there will always be conflict within us between the "flesh," or the sinful nature, and the Holy Spirit. "For the sinful nature desires what is contrary to the Spirit, and the Spirit what is contrary to the sinful nature. They are in conflict with each other, so that you do not do what you want" (Galatians 5:17).

Think of yourself walking into a room where the lighting is controlled by a dimmer switch. As you walk in, the lighting is dim and you see the furniture all in place, no newspapers lying around, and no dirty cups on the coffee table. The room looks neat and clean. But as you turn up the wattage in the lights, you begin to see dust on the furniture, smudges on the walls, chips in the paint, and threadbare spots in the carpet. The room that looked all right in the dim light suddenly appears dirty and unattractive under the full glare of the brighter light.

That is what happens in the life of a person who is pursuing holiness. At first your life may appear fairly good because you've been a decent sort of person and there are no gross sins that are visible. Then the Holy Spirit begins to "turn up the wattage" of His Word and reveal the more subtle, "refined" sins of which you were not even aware. Or perhaps you were aware of certain thoughts or actions but had not realized they were sinful.

Newly discovered sins usually dismay us. And the more holy a person is, the more he or she is dismayed. Then as we attempt to deal with these sins, we discover that they are stubbornly entrenched in our habits of life and are not easily dislodged.

Does this mean that we are no better off than the unbeliever who struggles with some habit? By no means. John Murray wrote, "Though sin still remains it does not have the mastery." Sin is like a defeated army in a civil war that, instead of surrendering and laying down its arms, simply fades into the countryside, from which it continues to wage a guerrilla war of harassment and sabotage against the government forces. Sin as a reigning power is defeated in the life of the believer, but it will *never* surrender. It will continue to harass us and seek to sabotage our Christian lives as long as we live.

The way the Spirit operates in our lives to sanctify us is shrouded in mystery. Paul said He works in us "to will and to act according to his good purpose" (Philippians 2:13), but he never tells us just how the Holy Spirit interacts with, or works on, our human spirit. I like to know how things work, and I used to try to figure out how the Holy Spirit interacts with our spirit, but I finally realized it was a futile pursuit.

However, the Holy Spirit does use understandable means to sanctify us. Some of these means, such as adversities and the exhortation and encouragement of others, are outside of our control to initiate. With other means, such as the learning and application of Scripture and the frequent use of prayer, He expects us to take the initiative.

I want to focus on the one specific means that Paul mentions in 2 Corinthians 3:18, that is, beholding the glory of Christ. Paul wrote, "But we all, with unveiled face beholding as in a mirror the glory of the Lord, are being transformed" (NASB). That is, beholding the glory of the Lord is one means the Spirit uses to transform us.

What is the glory of the Lord that Paul referred to, and how does beholding it transform us? First, the glory of the Lord denotes the presence of God and all that He is—His infiniteness, eternalness, holiness, sovereignty, goodness, etc. However, in the context of 2 Corinthians 3:18, Paul was contrasting the glory of the law given by Moses with the far-surpassing glory of the gospel.

This close connection between the gospel and Christ's glory leads me to believe that Paul was in this instance thinking of the glory of Christ, especially as it is revealed in the gospel. The law reveals the glory of God in His righteousness; the gospel reveals the glory of God in *both* His righteousness and grace.

This then is the glory that has a transforming effect on us. It is the glory of Christ revealed in the gospel, the good news that Jesus died in our place as our representative to free us not only from the penalty of sin but also from its dominion. A clear understanding and appropriation of the gospel, which gives freedom from sin's guilt and sin's grip, is, in the hands of the Holy Spirit, a chief means of sanctification.

To the degree that we feel we are on a legal or performance relationship with God, to that degree our progress in sanctification is impeded. A legal mode of thinking gives indwelling sin an advantage, because nothing cuts the nerve of the desire to pursue holiness as much as a sense of guilt. On the contrary, nothing so motivates us to deal with sin in our lives as does the understanding and application of the two truths that our sins are forgiven and the dominion of sin is broken because of our union with Christ.

Our specific responsibility in the pursuit of holiness as seen in 2 Corinthians 3:18, then, is to behold the glory of the Lord as it is displayed in the gospel. The gospel is the "mirror" through which we now behold His beauty. One day we shall see Christ, not as in a mirror, but face to face. Until then we behold Him in the gospel. Therefore, we must "preach the gospel to ourselves every day."**99**

DEVELOPING THE DISCIPLINE OF GRACE

1. At the beginning of the sanctification process, God replaces our stone hearts with hearts of flesh. What do you think it means to have a heart of flesh, as opposed to one of stone?

2. Why can't the Holy Spirit make any progress with a stone-hearted person?

3. a. The Holy Spirit's goal is to make us like Christ. You could choose virtually any story in the Gospels that portrays Christ and say to yourself, "God wants to make me like this." For example, read Mark 1:40-42. What does this paragraph tell you about what the Spirit intends you to become?

61

b. How do you feel when you consider that this is part of God's agenda for you? (Intimidated? Excited? Skeptical? Confident?) Explain.

4. On a scale of 1 (not at all) to 5 (always), indicate the extent to which you are conformed to the character of Christ, as measured in the following statements.

I hate sin in my own life, because of the despicable nature of it, not because I worry about what others would think.

1   2   3   4   5

My entire goal is to do the will of God, no matter how inconvenient or unpleasant that may seem to be at the time, simply because it is *His* will.

1   2   3   4   5

Not only have I stopped lying, cheating, gossiping, and thinking impure thoughts, but my speech and thought-life are focused on others' well-being.

1   2   3   4   5

I aim to please God and edify others in all that I say and do, rather than just getting through life as comfortably as I can.

1   2   3   4   5

5. Think of yourself in the room described above, in which the lighting is controlled by a dimmer switch. What are some sins in your life that you see now that you didn't notice when you first committed yourself to Christ?

6. a. How does beholding the glory of Christ in the gospel help to transform us?

b. In practical terms, how do we go about beholding Christ's glory in the gospel?

7. a. On your own, write down an area of sin in your life on which the Holy Spirit has been shining His spotlight.

b. Consider your answer to question 6b. How could you apply it to the area of sin you just named?

8. In your struggles with sin, do you find it personally helpful to remind yourself that sin is a defeated enemy? Why, or why not?

9. Close in prayer by reflecting on the transformation process you are experiencing. Tell God what you still struggle with. Thank Him for exposing this problem area and for defeating sin and death on the cross.

WHAT'S THE POINT OF ALL THIS?
Our specific responsibility in the pursuit of holiness, as seen in 2 Corinthians 3:18, is to behold the glory of the Lord as it is displayed in the gospel. To behold the glory of Christ in the gospel is a discipline of grace. In later sessions we will be looking at other disciplines that we must practice in the pursuit of holiness. Meditate on Matthew 22:36-40 and read chapter 7 of *The Discipline of Grace* in preparation for the next session.

7

OBEYING THE GREAT COMMANDMENT

"Teacher, which is the greatest commandment in the Law?"
Jesus replied: "'Love the Lord your God with all your heart
and with all your soul and with all your mind.' This is the
first and greatest commandment. And the second is like it:
'Love your neighbor as yourself.' All the Law and the
Prophets hang on these two commandments."
MATTHEW 22:36-40

CENTRAL IDEA

To love God with all my heart and soul and mind obviously means to love Him with all my being, with everything I have. To the degree that we live with an abiding sense of His love for us in Christ, to that degree will we love God with all our heart and soul and mind.

IDENTIFYING THE ISSUES

Excerpted and adapted from *The Discipline of Grace*, pages 111-125.

❝I enjoy fellowship with God, and often in the morning I awaken with the words in my mind, "I love You, Lord." For a time, however, it seemed as if God were saying, "Oh, really?" So I reflected on the question, What does it mean to love God?

I began to study what Jesus said in Matthew 22:36-40, plus Deuteronomy 6:1-9, the context from which Jesus draws this greatest commandment. One thing became clear: Obedience to God is primary. All manner of reminder devices keep His commands continually before us. Of course, the most obvious reminder device is the discipline of Scripture memorization. Daily review and meditation on key passages is far and away the most effective means of keeping God's commands continually before us.

In the midst of this strong emphasis to the Jews on obedience to God's Law and on the practical necessity of keeping its precepts always before them so they would obey, we find the greatest commandment, "Love the LORD your God with all your heart and with all your soul and with all your strength" (Deuteronomy 6:5). Whatever else might be involved in loving God with all my heart, obedience to His law is certainly a major part of it.

So what is new? What did I learn from my study of the "greatest commandment" that I didn't know before? What I saw was the intensity and wholeheartedness with which I should obey God.

However, most believers practice what I call a "cruise-control" approach to obedience. Many cars today have a convenient feature called cruise control. When you are driving on the highway you can accelerate to your desired speed, push the cruise-control button, and take your foot from the accelerator pedal. A mechanism attached to the engine will then maintain your desired speed, and you can ease back and relax a little. You don't have to watch your speedometer. You won't get a ticket for speeding, nor will you feel as tired.

Cruise control is a great feature on cars, but a lousy feature if characterizing our obedience to God. To continue the driving analogy, we press the accelerator pedal of obedience until we have brought our behavior up to a certain level or "speed." The level of obedience is most often determined by the behavior standard of other Christians around us. We don't want to lag behind them because we want to be as spiritual as they are. At the same time, we're not eager to forge ahead of them because we wouldn't want to be different. We want to just comfortably blend in with the level of obedience of those around us.

Once we have arrived at this comfortable level of obedience, we push the "cruise-control" button in our hearts, ease back, and relax. Our particular Christian culture then takes over and keeps us going at the accepted level of conduct. We don't have to watch the speed-limit signs in God's Word, and we certainly don't have to experience the fatigue that comes with seeking to obey Him with all our heart, soul, and mind. This then is what I call "cruise-control" obedience, and I fear it is descriptive of so many of us much, if not all, of the time.

By contrast, consider race-car drivers. They wouldn't think of using a cruise control or blending in with the speed of those around them. They are not out for a Sunday afternoon drive. They want to win the race. Race-car drivers are totally focused on their driving. Their foot is always on the accelerator as they try to push their car to the outer limits of its mechanical ability and endurance. Their eye is always on the track as they press to its limit their own skill in negotiating the turns on the track and the hazards of other cars around them. They are driving with all their heart, soul, and mind.

That's what it means to love God with all our heart and soul and mind and strength. The Apostle Paul didn't have auto races and cruise controls to use as illustrations, so he used the metaphor of a footrace (1 Corinthians 9:24-27).

The footracer running aimlessly or the boxer beating the air is equivalent to the Sunday driver with cruise control on. The runner striving for the prize who goes into strict training and beats his or her body—that is, subdues its desires—is like the race-car driver who drives all out. Moses and Jesus and Paul all said this is the way we should live the Christian life and love the God we worship.

God is not impressed with our worship on Sunday morning at church if we are practicing "cruise-control" obedience the rest of the week. You may sing with reverent zest or great emotional fervor, but your worship is only as pleasing to God as the obedience that accompanies it.

Although obedience is the primary way we express our love to God, it is not the same as love. Love for God is the only acceptable motive for obedience to Him. This love may express itself in a reverence for Him and a desire to please Him, but those expressions must spring from love. Only conduct that arises from love is worthy of the name of obedience.

Our motive for obedience is just as important, probably more so, to God than the level of our performance. A person who struggles with some persistent sin but does so out of love for God is more pleasing to Him than the person who has no such struggle but is proud of his or her self-control. Of course, the person who obeys from a motive of love will be concerned about his or her performance. There will be a sincere desire and an earnest effort to please God in every area of life.

How then can we develop this love for God so that our obedience is prompted by love instead of some lesser motive? Our love for God can only be a response to His love for us (1 John 4:19). If I do not believe God loves me, I cannot love Him. To love God, I must believe that He is for me, not against me (Romans 8:31), and that He accepts me as a son or a daughter, not a slave (Galatians 4:7).

What would keep us from believing that God loves us? The answer is a sense of guilt and condemnation because of our sin. A tender conscience that is alert to sin, especially those "refined" sins such as pride, criticality, resentment, discontent, irritableness, and the like, is a great advantage in the pursuit of holiness, as it enables us to become aware of sins that lie deep beneath the level of external actions. But this same tender conscience can load us down with guilt, and when we are under that burden and sense of condemnation, it is difficult to love God or believe that He loves us.

This means that we must continually take those sins that our consciences accuse us of to the cross and plead the cleansing blood of Jesus. Only the blood of Christ cleanses our consciences so that we may no longer feel guilty (Hebrews 9:14, 10:2). The extent to which we realize and acknowledge our own sinfulness, and the extent to which we realize the total forgiveness and cleansing from those sins, will determine the measure of our love to God (Luke 7:47).

If we want to grow in our love for God and in the acceptable obedience that flows out of that love, we must keep coming back to the gospel before us every day. Because we sin every day and our consciences condemn us every day, we need the gospel every day.**❞**

DEVELOPING THE DISCIPLINE OF GRACE

1. Bridges contrasts "cruise control" obedience with "race car" obedience. What are some of the factors that you think typically keep believers from pursuing "race car" obedience?

2. Does your obedience tend to be more of the "cruise control" or "race car" variety? (Or do you spend a lot of time parked?) Why do you suppose this is the case?

3. Study Deuteronomy 6:1-9, which is the Old Testament context for the "greatest commandment" Jesus cites in Matthew 22:37. Note how words such as *commands*, *decrees*, and *laws* are prominent. How is obedience to these commands, decrees, and laws emphasized?

4. a. What are some innovative and effective ways of impressing God's commands, decrees, and laws on ourselves and our children? (Instead of tying the Scriptures on your hands and foreheads or writing them on your doorframes and gates, what do you do?)

❑ "Post-It" note with a pertinent verse of Scripture stuck on the bathroom mirror or the clock on my desk.

❑ A three-by-five card with a Scripture for the day written on it that I carry in my shirt pocket and refer to throughout the day.

❑ A card of Scripture taped on the dashboard or rearview mirror of my car.

❑ I practice the discipline of Scripture memorization, with daily review and meditation.

❑ Other (list some):

b. If you do not already have a habit of impressing Scripture on your mind, what approach (one of the above or another) appeals to you?

5. Equating obedience to God with love for God is a prominent feature of Deuteronomy. Without trying to be exhaustive, Bridges found six other passages in the book where love and obedience are tied together. To help us feel the impact of this strong repetitive emphasis, those Scriptures are quoted below. In each instance, what is the relationship of love for God and obedience to God?

❑ Now, O Israel, what does the LORD your God ask of you but to fear the LORD your God, to walk in all his ways, to love him, to serve the LORD your God with all your heart and with all your soul, and to observe the LORD's commands and decrees that I am giving you today for your own good? (10:12-13)

❑ So if you faithfully obey the commands I am giving you today—to love the LORD your God and to serve him with all your heart and with all your soul. (11:13)

❑ If you carefully observe all these commands I am giving you to follow—to love the LORD your God, to walk in all his ways and to hold fast to him. (11:22)

❑ Because you carefully follow all these laws I command you today—to love the LORD your God and to walk always in his ways. (19:9)

❑ The LORD your God will circumcise your hearts and the hearts of your descendants, so that you may love him with all your heart and with all your soul, and live. . . . You will again obey the LORD and follow all his commands I am giving you today. (30:6,8)

❑ This day I call heaven and earth as witnesses against you that I have set before you life and death, blessings and curses. Now choose life, so that you and your children may live and that you may love the LORD your God, listen to his voice, and hold fast to him. For the LORD is your life, and he will give you many years in the land he swore to give to your fathers, Abraham, Isaac and Jacob. (30:19-20)

6. Without the motive of love, my apparent obedience may be self-serving. Without love, we are motivated to do good, but for all the wrong reasons. To illustrate how our deceitful hearts can lead us to do something good from some motive other than love to God, we've cited a few examples here. Can you think of any recent examples from your experience that illustrate these reasons?

a. I may fear God will punish me, or at least withhold His blessing from me, because of some disobedience.

b. I may abstain from a particular sinful action out of fear I will be found out, not because I hate the sin that God hates.

c. I struggle against some temptation to avoid the guilt that follows, rather than out of love to God.

d. I may be seeking to earn God's blessing through some pious action—kneeling at prayer, having a daily quiet time, or something else equally subtle or superstitious.

e. I may conform to a certain standard of conduct because I want to fit in with and be accepted by the Christian culture in which I live.

f. I might even obey outwardly because I have a compliant personality, and it is simply my "nature" to obey my parents, or my teacher, or civil authorities, or even God.

g. I may do something outstanding for God, but my obedience is tainted with self-righteous pride in my accomplishment.

7. The Puritan John Owen wrote that the greatest sorrow and burden we can lay on God the Father is not to believe He loves us. Why is that a greater burden than committing some scandalous sin?

8. What in this session is personally relevant to you?

9. As you close in prayer, meditate on the truth of the gospel and let those thoughts move you to tell God how much you love Him.

WHAT'S THE POINT OF ALL THIS?

As we turn our attention in the following sessions to the personal disciplines we need to practice in the pursuit of holiness, let us not put the gospel "on the shelf" of our lives. Let us review it daily, and in the joy that it brings, pursue these disciplines.

Beginning with the next session we will consider some of the other disciplines we must practice that are important to the pursuit of holiness. But remember, none is more important than the discipline of continually feeding your soul on the great truth of the gospel. Meditate on Psalm 127:1 and read chapter 8 of *The Discipline of Grace* in preparation for the next session.

8

Dependent Discipline

Unless the LORD builds the house,
its builders labor in vain.
Unless the LORD watches over the city,
the watchmen stand guard in vain.

PSALM 127:1

CENTRAL IDEA

If we are to make any progress in the pursuit of holiness, we must assume our responsibility to discipline or train ourselves. But we must do this in total dependence on the Holy Spirit to work in us and strengthen us with the strength that is in Christ.

IDENTIFYING THE ISSUES

Excerpted and adapted from *The Discipline of Grace*, pages 127-143.

66Think of yourself seated in a jet passenger plane flying thirty-five thousand feet above the earth. As you look at the two wings you see the words *dependence* on the left wing and *discipline* on the right wing. This airplane illustrates one of the most important principles in the Christian life. Just as the airplane must have both wings to fly, so we must exercise both discipline and dependence in the pursuit of holiness. Just as it is impossible for an airplane to fly with only one wing, so it is impossible for us to successfully pursue holiness with only dependence or discipline. Discipline, as I am now using the word, refers to certain activities designed to train a person in a particular skill. The Apostle Paul exhorted Timothy to "train himself," or discipline himself, to be godly as if earnestly engaged in competitive athletic training (1 Timothy 4:7). Yet Paul certainly didn't envision a reliance on sheer human willpower. Rather, Paul urged Timothy to be strong in the grace—that is, the strength—that is in Christ Jesus (2 Timothy 2:1).

Today, we would tend to divide into two camps: the more "spiritual" people who call an all-night prayer meeting and the "practical" ones among us who get busy organizing and doing the church work. Nehemiah and his people did both. When under enemy attack he said, "We prayed to our God and posted a guard day and night to meet this threat" (Nehemiah 4:9).

There are instances in the Old Testament where God miraculously intervened and actually fought the battle for Israel. However, *there is not a single instance in New Testament teaching on holiness where we are taught to depend on the Holy Spirit without a corresponding exercise of discipline on our part.*

We often use the expression, "Let the Lord live His life through me." I am personally uncomfortable with this expression because it suggests a passivity on our part. He does not live His life through me. Rather, as I depend on Him, He enables *me* to live a life pleasing to Him.

This is far more than semantics. It is a difference in our understanding of how God works in us. The essence of the passive view (in fairness to those who teach this view of sanctification, they would call it a "faith" approach, not a passive approach) is summed up in a statement that goes something like this: Man's part is to trust; God's part is to work. The believer can do nothing but trust, while the God in whom he or she trusts does the work.

The idea that we can do *nothing* but trust is particularly

troubling to me. God's work does not make our effort unnecessary, but rather makes it effective. There is no question that we are responsible to pursue holiness with all the intensity that the word *pursue* implies. Every moral imperative in the Bible (e.g., "put to death the misdeeds of the body") addresses itself to our responsibility to discipline ourselves unto godliness. Consider, too, how Paul *labored* and *struggled*—literally, agonized "with all his energy" to do the work of ministry (Colossians 1:28-29). There is no question about the intensity of Paul's labors. He toiled to the point of weariness and he agonized like an athlete straining to break the tape, but he did so in the Lord's strength. To use our airplane illustration, he didn't try to fly with only one wing.

Sometimes we don't sense we are experiencing His strength. Instead we experience deep, agonizing failure. We may even weep over our sins and wonder why the Holy Spirit doesn't come to our aid and strengthen us against the onslaught of temptation (Romans 7:15). Whatever the reason, which we may never know, our responsibility is to utterly depend on Him. He sovereignly and with infinite wisdom determines how best to respond to our dependency.

Despite my concern about the so-called passive approach to holiness, I am just as concerned about the self-discipline approach. There is no doubt that disciplined people, both believers and unbelievers, can effect change in themselves. A major temptation in the self-discipline approach to holiness, however, is to rely on a regimen of spiritual disciplines instead of on the Holy Spirit.

We can plant and we can water, but we cannot make things grow; only the Holy Spirit can do that (1 Corinthians 3:7). Let's extend this farming metaphor to make a further point. There are six things farmers must do—plow, plant, fertilize, irrigate, cultivate, and harvest—and only two things they cannot do, namely, make crops grow and control the weather. They can even to a degree circumvent the weather by irrigating in case of drought. But the one thing they absolutely cannot do is the most critical of all.

76

Without the life that makes things grow, all their disciplines of farming are useless.

Just as typical farmers put their confidence in the performance of their duties, so we believers who take seriously our responsibility for holiness tend to put our confidence in the performance of our disciplines. Like farmers, we take for granted the spiritual life that makes us grow.

How then can we grow in a conscious sense of dependence on Christ? Through the discipline of prayer. Prayer is the tangible expression of our dependence. The writer of Psalm 119 teaches us about the discipline of prayer in the pursuit of holiness. Twenty-two times the psalmist prays to God for help in obeying His law (e.g., 119:11-16,33-37).

The psalmist stored up God's Word in his heart. He recounted it to others, he rejoiced in obeying it, he meditated on it, he delighted in it, and he did not neglect it. The psalmist was not only a man of discipline but also a man of prayer. His discipline did not cause him to neglect prayer for God to work, nor did his prayer cause him to neglect his own work. He practiced discipline *and* dependence.

Our prayers of dependence should be of two types: planned periods of prayer and unplanned, spontaneous prayer. We see both in the life of Nehemiah (especially chapters 1–2). Since he prayed over a period of several months, this part of Nehemiah's prayer life was *planned, protracted, persevering* prayer. It was planned because it was made a part of his daily schedule, protracted because it extended over a period of several months, and persevering because he continued to pray until God answered. Yet when the moment of crisis arrived to face the king with his sorrow, Nehemiah "prayed to the God of heaven, and [he] answered the king" (2:4-5). In contrast to his prayer over the previous few months, this prayer was *unplanned, short,* and *spontaneous.*

Like Nehemiah, we need these unplanned, short, spontaneous prayers. We need them throughout the day as we face temptations to sin and as we encounter circumstances in which we need help to display godly character.

Whatever the situation, a quick "Lord, help me" focuses our dependence upon God instead of our own willpower and brings the Spirit's aid to us. He does withhold His aid when we forget our need of it and do not ask Him for it.

This admission of helplessness and dependence is repugnant to our sinful spirit of self-sufficiency. So if we want to become holy we must pursue, not a spirit of independence, but a spirit of dependence. And one of the best means God has given us for doing this is the discipline of prayer. 🙨

DEVELOPING THE DISCIPLINE OF GRACE

1. Think of the two wings of the airplane, discipline and dependence. In what proportion do they exist in your life?

❑ My pursuit of holiness tilts toward the passive ("faith") approach.
❑ My pursuit of holiness is more like the self-disciplined ("works") approach.
❑ My life is unbalanced, as if I am flying on one wing, soon to fall.
❑ I'm weak in both wings.
❑ I think I am fairly well balanced between discipline and dependence.
❑ Other (describe it):

2. Often in the Scriptures the concepts of both dependence and responsibility appear in the same sentence or paragraph. For each of the examples below, tell how the passage affirms *dependence* and how it affirms *discipline*.

Psalm 119:11-16

John 15:4-5

Philippians 4:11-13

Colossians 1:28-29

3. Think of a challenge to growth that you are currently facing, such as raising your children well or handling an ethical dilemma at work.

    a. What will it look like for you to exercise *dependence* in this situation?

    b. What will it look like for you to bring *discipline* to bear in this situation?

4. Reflect on a time when you were not sensing God's strength during some deep need or agonizing failure. The Holy Spirit doesn't always strengthen us in such times in a way that enables us to triumph. Why do you think He didn't in your case?

   ❏ God was letting me see the sinfulness of my own heart.
   ❏ God was causing me to realize how weak I am in myself and how dependent on Him I really am.

❑ God was curbing a tendency toward spiritual pride and causing me to grow in humility.
❑ Other (name a possibility):

5. The publishing industry has foisted on us a plethora of self-help books, many of which are excellent aids to personal growth and training, albeit from a secular point of view. The problem with such books comes when they tempt us to rely on a regimen of disciplines instead of on the Holy Spirit. This temptation can happen with Christian self-help books (even this one), as well as with secular books.

a. Name one book you have read, Christian or secular, whose principles you have actually applied and seen cause change in your life.

b. In applying these principles of self-discipline, were you trusting in God to work, or were you trusting in the plan or techniques to work?

c. Is there anything you would do differently now regarding self-help books? Explain.

6. You believe in the work of the Holy Spirit and you give lip service to this need for dependence in Sunday worship, but do you truly practice it each day?

❑ Throughout the day, every day of the week, I acknowledge my dependence on Him.
❑ I mostly pursue holiness in the strength of my own willpower and a very disciplined life.

❑ My prayer life is meager or perfunctory, which is to say, in effect, I can handle most of my spiritual life somehow on my own.

❑ My reliance on the Holy Spirit has increased substantially during the past year.

❑ I must admit I'm not even committed to the pursuit of holiness.

❑ Other (describe your situation):

7. Both types of prayer—*planned* and *spontaneous*—were needed in Nehemiah's situation. We can learn from Nehemiah's example how to pray for ourselves in the pursuit of holiness. Which type of prayer are you more inclined to do?

❑ I usually persist in planned, protracted prayer until God answers.

❑ I usually plunge into the crisis situation and pray quick, silent, spontaneous prayers at the time of greatest need.

❑ I usually pray in panoramic fashion—once at the outset of the day for everything to simply "pan out" as hoped for.

❑ What, me pray? Why pray when you can worry?

❑ Other (explain):

8. Unless you *plan* to pray and set aside a specific *time* to do it, you will invariably fail to carry out your good intentions. So if you do not already have this practice, why not stop to make your plan now? What time will you set aside each day for the next week to pray? It helps to write your plan on paper.

The agenda for your prayer time should include asking God to enable you to become free of persistent sins (e.g., gossip; irritability; impatience; lack of love; impure thoughts; and undisciplined, wandering eyes) and grow in specific virtues of Christian character. Note that your prayer is for the Spirit to *enable* you to do these things; you are the one who must act, but the Spirit must enable you.

9. Take a few minutes for prayer at the end of your group meeting to express to God your dependence upon Him. You could let each group member complete this sentence: "Lord, I acknowledge that I am dependent on You for . . . , and I thank You that I can rely on You for this."

WHAT'S THE POINT OF ALL THIS?
We need to set aside time each day for *planned, protracted, persevering* prayer, as well as the spontaneous prayers demanded by each situation we come across. This is the discipline of dependence. Next session we focus on the discipline of commitment. Before we are finished, you will end up with about six disciplines. But remember, none is more important than the discipline of dependence, the one weighty wing which balances the other six lined up on the other wing.

Meditate on Psalm 119:106 and read chapter 9 of *The Discipline of Grace* in preparation for the next session.

9

THE DISCIPLINE OF COMMITMENT

I have taken an oath and confirmed it,
that I will follow your righteous laws.
PSALM 119:106

CENTRAL IDEA

If we hope to make any progress in the pursuit of holiness, commitment is essential. One reason we do not see more progress in holiness in our lives is because we have for the most part lost sight of the necessity of commitment.

IDENTIFYING THE ISSUES

Excerpted and adapted from *The Discipline of Grace*, pages 145-160.

66No one ever reaches the Olympic Games without a commitment to the rigorous training required to reach that level of performance. When the Apostle Paul urged Timothy to train himself to be godly (1 Timothy 4:7), he used a word from the athletic world of that time. Paul knew that the pursuit of holiness requires that same high level of commitment.

When Paul turned his attention to practical issues of Christian living, the first thing he did was call for commitment. Whereas the athlete's commitment is to himself or herself or perhaps to the team, the commitment Paul urges upon us is to God. Offer your body to Him as "instruments of righteousness," that is, as a "living sacrifice," holy and pleasing to Him (Romans 6:13,19; 12:1).

When we commit ourselves to the pursuit of holiness, we need to insure that our commitment is actually to God, not simply to a holy lifestyle or a set of moral values. We should not seek holiness in order to feel good about ourselves, or to blend in with our Christian peer group, or to avoid the sense of shame and guilt that follows the committing of persistent sin.

For example, a lack of self-control in subjecting ourselves to unworthy habits may be disappointing to us and cause us to lose self-esteem, but realize how this "besetting sin" also grieves God. We cannot control what our eyes look at, what our mouth speaks, or what our hands and feet do if our whole being, including our mind and heart, is not committed to God.

Such a commitment must allow for no exceptions, no secret sins we want to hold onto, no sinful habits we are unwilling to give up. *We must make it our aim not to sin.* This doesn't mean we can arrive at sinless perfection in this life, for even our best deeds are stained with sin. But it does mean our firm intention must be not to sin willfully. There is no point in praying for God's help in the face of temptation if we have not made a commitment to obedience without exception.

The psalmist felt so strongly about his commitment to obedience that he took an oath that he would "follow [God's] righteous laws" (Psalm 119:106). An oath, in this context, is a solemn calling on God to witness that the person sincerely intends to do what he or she says. It is a declaration or promise to fulfill a pledge, a commitment of the highest level.

Is it your intention to please God in all your actions? If not, you will constantly find yourself making exceptions. You will have a "just one more time" syndrome. This "one more time" manner of thinking undermines our commitment. Every time we give in to a temptation, even though it may seem small to us, we make it easier to give in the next time. Sin has a tendency to exert an ever-increasing power on us if it is not resisted on every occasion (Romans 6:19).

It does not matter whether the sin to which we are tempted is seemingly small or large. The principle we are looking at—that saying yes to *any* temptation weakens our commitment to resist sin—works in either case.

Just as we need to make a commitment not to sin willfully, so we need to make a commitment to put on the positive virtues of Christian character. It is not enough to stop cheating on one's income-tax return; we must also learn to share with those in need. It is not enough to avoid being bitter against those who have wronged us; we need to forgive as God has forgiven us. It is not enough to pray that God will enable us to deal with a volatile temper; we must also ask Him to help us put on compassion and kindness.

The tradesman should commit himself to operate his business, not in such a way as to make the most money, but in such a way as to be most pleasing to God. The same principle of commitment applies to how the student approaches his or her studies, to the way we do our buying, to the way we compete in games, to the way we decorate our houses and keep our lawns, and even to the way we drive.

In addition to an overall commitment to pursue holiness in every area of life, I find it helpful to make specific commitments in areas where I am particularly prone to sin. For example, if someone is prone to gossip or to speak critically of others, it is helpful to make a specific commitment to stop those practices.

We find two examples of specific commitments in the lives of Job and Daniel. Job's commitment concerned lustful looks, so he singled out this specific area of temptation, "making a covenant with my eyes" (Job 31:1). Daniel's commitment was not to eat food that would violate the dietary laws God had established for Israel (Daniel 1:8).

Job's temptation to look lustfully at a girl arose from the sinfulness of his own heart. Daniel's temptation came from the environment or circumstances in which he found himself. *We are vulnerable to both kinds of temptations.* People will help you compromise your integrity if you have not already made a commitment to be absolutely honest in your business dealings.

I urge you, before you finish this reading, to stop and list any areas of temptation wherein you need to make a specific commitment. In fact, you may find you will need to make several commitments—sins to put off or avoid and Christlike traits to put on. If you do not commit yourself to the pursuit of holiness in these specific areas of your life, you will find a tendency to vacillate in the face of these temptations.

I suspect the overall flavor of this chapter may seem too rigorous and even legalistic to some people. "Who," they may ask, "can possibly keep such a commitment to a pursuit of holiness without exception for even some 'small' sins? And if there are no exceptions, is there any place for grace? Is God really this strict?"

Yes, God really is this strict, because He cannot compromise His holiness the least bit. His goal is to conform us to the likeness of His Son, and Jesus was completely without sin, though He was tempted in every way that we are (Hebrews 4:15). No, we cannot, or perhaps will not, keep these commitments perfectly, but keeping them perfectly should at least be our aim. In a battle, some soldiers will always be hit, but every one of them makes it his aim not to be hit.

Is there any place for grace? Most assuredly; in fact, the Apostle Paul based his call for such decisive commitment (in Romans 6:13 and 12:1) on God's mercy or grace. Whether it is grace viewed as God's undeserved favor, as we would understand it in Romans 12:1, or viewed as God's divine enabling, as we should understand it in the context of Romans 6:13, such grace is the basis for our commitment to pursue holiness. What Paul asked for from us is only a response of love and gratitude, which expresses itself in loving commitment.

While an all-out, nothing-held-back commitment to the pursuit of holiness may be exhausting, it will not be oppressive if it is grounded in grace. But to be grounded in grace, it must be continually referred back to the gospel. So don't just preach the gospel to yourself every day merely to experience the cleansing of your conscience. Use the occasion of hearing the gospel to reaffirm your loving commitment to Him. **99**

DEVELOPING THE DISCIPLINE OF GRACE

1. Put yourself in this cartoon:

> You're about to leap from the ledge of a high-rise apartment building with a suicide note in hand but with a parachute strapped to your back. Your wife, leaning out of the window, says to you, "Just can't make a commitment to anything—can you, Larry?"

    a. Although intended to be humorous, the cartoon makes a serious point. What are some commitments you have made, or intended to make, during the past year or so?

    b. How faithful have you been to those commitments? In what ways have you hedged your bets or failed to follow through?

2. This chapter poses quite a challenge: to present our bodies as living sacrifices; to take an oath to obey God's righteous laws; to resolve to allow no exceptions to our

obedience. How do you respond to that call to commitment?

❑ I'm struck by the impossibility of totally keeping such a commitment.

❑ I am reluctant to make a commitment I know I will not keep.

❑ I am willing to make pleasing God in all ways my aim or goal in life.

❑ I am content to remain on "cruise-control" obedience and merely avoid scandalous sin and not worry about the "refined" sins that I consider unimportant.

❑ I want to aggressively pursue holiness like the race car driver who is totally focused on winning and finishing the race, going all out for God.

❑ Other (describe your response):

3. Some sins come as a result of the environment in which we live or work. If most used-car dealers turn back the odometers of cars taken as trade-ins, then a Christian car dealer who renounces this unethical practice will be at a disadvantage relative to his competitors.

   a. What temptations do you face in your school or work?

   b. When have you paid the price for being a Christian and acted ethically in one of those tempting situations?

c. When have you given in to a temptation because "everyone does it"? (You can answer this question privately, sharing your answer with your group only if you know one another well.)

4. What are some areas in which you need to make some specific commitments to resist sin or show Christlikeness? Ask the Holy Spirit to make His list apparent to you. Again, this list will be for your eyes only so you can review it and pray over it daily.

   a. Do you need to make a covenant with your eyes about what you look at? If so, explain.

   b. Do you need to covenant with your mouth about what you say? Explain.

   c. What about with your mind about what you think? Explain.

   d. Is there a particular temptation that arises in your work or school?

   e. Is there a particular area in your marriage or in your relationship with your children, your parents, or even a friend, or with an associate at work, where you are not demonstrating the Spirit's fruit of love, patience, or kindness?

f. What else would you add to this list?

You may find you will need to make several commitments—sins to put off or avoid and Christlike traits to put on. If you do not commit yourself to the pursuit of holiness in these specific areas of your life, you will tend to waver in the face of these temptations.

Take a moment to tell the Holy Spirit of your commitments and ask Him to enable you to keep them.

5. With your group, discuss this exercise of listing your commitments. (How do you feel after having made these commitments? Do you expect yourself to follow through? What will be your major obstacles to following through, and what will you do about those obstacles?)

6. Lest the reader get the wrong impression and give up in despair at ever following through on such commitments, Bridges reminds us that the discipline of commitment is always called for in the context of the gospel of grace. See Romans 6:13 and 12:1 in context. How does this grace relate to the discipline of commitment?

7. a. Last session we invited you to read part of Psalm 119, noting where the psalmist prays to God for help in obeying His law. Now read through all of Psalm 119, this time looking for expressions of the psalmist's vow or pledge of commitment. To what does he commit himself?

b. Does the psalmist's commitment suggest any similar commitments the Lord might be calling and enabling you to make? Explain.

8. With your group, express to God your dependence on Him to enable you to keep your commitments. You could have just one person pray or give each group member an opportunity to pray for the ability to follow through.

WHAT'S THE POINT OF ALL THIS?

This discipline of commitment complements and is fulfilled by the discipline of dependence. Without commitment, progress in the pursuit of holiness is not possible. Next session we focus on the discipline of convictions. Meditate on Romans 12:2 and read chapter 10 of *The Discipline of Grace* in preparation for the next session.

10

THE DISCIPLINE OF CONVICTIONS

Do not conform any longer to the pattern of this world,
but be transformed by the renewing of your mind.
Then you will be able to test and approve what
God's will is—his good, pleasing and perfect will.

ROMANS 12:2

CENTRAL IDEA

We cannot effectively pursue holiness without the Word of God stored up in our minds where it can be used by the Holy Spirit to transform us. We need the discipline of forming Bible-based convictions.

IDENTIFYING THE ISSUES

Excerpted and adapted from *The Discipline of Grace*, pages 161-180.

❝It should not surprise us that society in general has moved in the direction of ancient Israel when "every man did that which was right in his own eyes" (Judges 21:25, KJV). Western civilization has deliberately turned away from the Bible as its moral authority. Now we are suffering the consequences.

What should disturb us, however, is that evangelicals are moving in the same direction. Forty percent decide for themselves what is right and wrong instead of going to the

Bible. No wonder there is often little difference between the ethical views and behavior of professing Christians and those who have nothing to do with Christianity. Morality becomes merely a matter of one's personal opinion.

In many evangelical circles we have morality and sanctification by consensus. We live according to the standard of conduct of Christians around us. We expect to become holy by osmosis, by the absorption of the ethical values of our Christian peer group.

If we are going to make progress in the pursuit of holiness, we must aim to live according to the precepts of Scripture—not according to the culture, even Christian culture, around us. But how can we do this if we don't know what those precepts are? It is not sufficient for us to hear one or two thirty-minute sermons a week. We must be exposed to the Scriptures daily if we hope to live under their authority.

To pursue holiness, one of the disciplines we must become skilled in is the development of *Bible-based convictions*. A conviction is something you believe so strongly that it affects the way you live. Our convictions and values will come from society around us (the world), or they will come as our minds are renewed by the Word of God. There is no third option, according to the Apostle Paul, who contrasted conforming (or being conformed) to the pattern of this world and being transformed by the renewal of one's mind (Romans 12:2).

Likewise, the writer of Psalm 1 envisions two diametrically opposing camps, or two alternative groups of people, one of which we are. Some are being drawn more and more under the controlling influence of wicked people, until at last they themselves begin to influence others. The second group are those who delight in the law of God and meditate on it, or think about it continually. Again, we are being influenced by the forces of sinful society, or we are being influenced by the life-changing Word of God. There is no neutral sphere of influence.

The truth is, of course, that we believers are probably

being influenced by both society and the Word of God. Whether one or the other is more influential depends on what we meditate on consistently and habitually. Thinking is our most constant activity; we are never without thoughts. But we can choose the direction and content of those thoughts.

Meditation on Scripture is a *discipline*. We must commit ourselves to be proactive. We must memorize key passages (or carry them on cards) so that we can think about them. We must be alert for those times during the day when we can turn our minds to the Word of God, and then we must *do* it. Even the practice of daily Bible reading is insufficient if we go the rest of the day without meditating on some truths of Scripture. We must choose to meditate instead of thinking about other things, or listening to the radio, or watching television.[1]

If we do not *actively* seek to come under the influence of God's Word, we *will* come under the influence of sinful society around us. The impact of our culture with its heavy emphasis on materialism, living for one's self, and instant gratification is simply too strong and pervasive for us not to be influenced by it.

We are to be *transformed* by the renewing of our minds (Romans 12:2). The word *transformed* denotes a deep internal change in our character, or heart, that produces outward change in our behavior (2 Corinthians 3:18). Jesus said that it is "from within, out of men's hearts," that evil thoughts and actions come (Mark 7:21). A changed heart does not continue to produce such evil.

The verb *be transformed* in Romans 12:2 and 2 Corinthians 3:18 is an exhortation. Paul does not urge us to transform something else, but to have some transforming action done *to us*. Consider the case of little Tommy who comes in from his ball game grimy with sweat and dirt. His mother takes one look at Tommy and says, "Go take a shower." That's a command with an active verb. Tommy's mother wants him to be made clean, so she directs him to take a shower, which brings him under the cleansing

94

action of soap and water. Just as Tommy cannot cleanse himself (left to his own devices, he'd only rearrange the dirt), so also we cannot transform ourselves. Only the Holy Spirit can do that. As Tommy must bring himself under the cleansing action of the soap and water, so we must bring ourselves under the transforming action of the Holy Spirit.

This means, of course, that we must continually submit our minds to the Word of God, which is the chief instrument the Holy Spirit uses to transform us. Paul's exhortation to be transformed is in the present tense, implying a continuous process that should be occurring every day of our lives. Thus we begin to develop Bible-based convictions. It is more than just our thoughts and understanding that need to be changed. We must also be changed in our affections and wills.

However knowledgeable about Scripture we may be, we need to approach it each day as little children, asking the Holy Spirit to teach us. Approach the Scriptures in humility and expect the Holy Spirit to humble you even further as you continue to be taught by Him from His Word. This takes a certain mental discipline and effective methods of Bible study, but common to all of them is an attitude of dependent diligence. Solomon defined diligent study as "applying your heart to understanding" and looking for it "as for silver" or "hidden treasure" (Proverbs 2:2,4).

Along with an attitude of diligence, we also need an attitude of dependence. "Calling out" and "crying aloud" (2:3) denote an almost desperate sense of dependence, not the usual perfunctory prayer for God to teach us as we begin our weekly Bible study.

The Lord does not reward perfunctory lip service, indolence, or sinful self-confidence in Bible study—only diligence and dependence. Acquiring more knowledge of biblical truth is not the point; developing life-changing convictions is the point of our Bible study. In fact, the mere acquisition of Bible facts or doctrinal truth without application to one's life of godliness can lead to spiritual pride.

So pray for knowledge of truth that will change lives rather than simply inform minds. Such spiritual wisdom is more profitable than silver, yields better returns than gold, and is more precious than rubies (Proverbs 3:13-15).

We can not develop Bible-based convictions merely by storing up Bible knowledge in our heads. We do not even develop them by personal Bible study and Scripture memorization, though those practices certainly help us get started. Convictions are really developed when we begin to *apply* the teachings of Scripture to real-life situations (James 1:22). **99**

DEVELOPING THE DISCIPLINE OF GRACE

1. We are to "store up" God's precious Word within us (Psalm 119:11; Proverbs 2:1, 7:1). The idea behind "store up" is to lay away in anticipation of a future need or opportunity. People store up canned fruits and vegetables from their garden, a "rainy day" fund from their paper route, or an old penny collection from their grandparents.

   a. In your younger days, what did you so value that you stored it up, treasuring it, perhaps even to this day?

   b. If you were to apply that same diligence and child-like zeal to Bible study or Scripture memorization, valuing it above everything else (Proverbs 3:13-15), what do you think would be the result five years from now?

2. Someone has observed, "A belief is what you hold, but a conviction is what holds you." You may live contrary to what you believe, but you cannot live contrary to

your convictions. In developing our convictions, we believers are influenced by both society and the Word of God. What determines whether we are influenced by one more than the other?

3. a. Below are two contrary convictions. Which one do you tend to live by more than the other? Give an example of how you have displayed that conviction in your behavior.

❑ Avoid pain if at all possible.
❑ If doing what Christ would do involves pain, then I have through the Holy Spirit the strength to endure that pain.

b. What do you think it would take for the second of these two convictions to become the one you live by habitually?

4. The idea of continually meditating on the Word of God may seem unrealistic and unattainable in our busy age when our minds need to be occupied with the various responsibilities we all have. So the question naturally arises: "How can I meditate on Scripture, when I have to think about my work all day long?" What opportunities to meditate on Scripture does your day offer you?

5. When your mind is free to wander where does it go? (Or, what do you think about in your free time?)

❑ My mind turns to Scripture.
❑ I think about my problems.
❑ I engage in mental arguing with a personal nemesis.
❑ I allow my mind to drift into a wasteland of impure thoughts.
❑ I hum tunes from my favorite songs.
❑ Other (give an example):

6. What value do you place upon the Word of God in practice?

❑ I study the Bible only because I know it is something Christians should do.
❑ I depend more on study aids, Bible commentaries, and my intellect than on the Holy Spirit to enlighten my understanding of Scripture.
❑ I search the Scriptures with the same childlike intensity that I use when searching for "hidden treasures" or my favorite collectibles.
❑ Like my storehouse of favorite collectibles, God's Word remains on the shelf, collecting dust.
❑ Other:

7. God provides opportunities to develop Bible-based convictions by applying the teachings of Scripture to real-life situations, such as the following:

My wife and I recently went shopping for a coffee table. We had agreed on the style we wanted and very quickly found one at a price within our range. I like to buy as soon as I find what I like, but my wife is a "shopper." She likes to look at everything in the store. Sure enough, she soon came upon her "dream" coffee table, a rather uncommon design that was more expensive. I started talking about being good stewards of the money God has given us, but God started "talking" to me (through the convicting work of His Spirit) about husbands loving their wives just as Christ loved the Church (Ephesians 5:25). As I worked through that situation, I realized one of the concrete ways to love my wife was to be more sensitive to her dreams and desires. In that situation God desired that I learn to apply Ephesians 5:25 to a real-life situation, and thus be a loving husband of my wife, not just a good steward of His resources.

Describe a situation in which God gave you a chance to build a conviction by applying the teaching of Scripture.

8. During the coming week, pray as the psalmist did that God will open your eyes to see wonderful things in His law, and that He will give you understanding so as to keep His law (Psalm 119:18,34). He will also very likely make you aware of areas of your life where you are not fully obedient to His revealed will.

9. Jesus used Scripture to combat temptation (Matthew 4:1-11). In session 9 we urged you to make specific commitments regarding your areas of vulnerability to sin. How can you go about finding passages of Scripture that apply to these vulnerabilities so that you can memorize those passages and use them when temptation strikes? (If you don't already know where in the Bible to find relevant passages, is there someone you can ask for suggestions? Have you read a book that mentions relevant passages? Can you start reading through the New Testament, looking for passages that apply to your need? Describe your plan.)

10. Use Psalm 119:18,34 as the basis for prayer with your group at the end of your discussion.

WHAT'S THE POINT OF ALL THIS?

We have looked at some difficult disciplines in this session: diligent but dependent Bible study, Scripture memorization, continual meditation, and application of Scripture to real-life situations. Actually, these disciplines are not all that difficult, but they can appear that way to those who have never practiced them. So the question may arise in some minds, Is there any room for grace here? What happens if I stumble along in Scripture memorization, for example?

First of all, God does not love us any less. His love for us is based solely on the fact that we are in union with His Son Jesus Christ. The discipline of developing Bible-based convictions (Romans 12:2) should be a response to the mercy and grace of God to us through Christ (Romans 12:1).

Next session we focus on the discipline of choices. Meditate on Romans 6:19 and read chapter 11 of *The Discipline of Grace* in preparation for the next session.

NOTE
1. I am much aware that Scripture memorization has largely fallen by the wayside in our day of microwave meals and television entertainment. I know this requires work and is sometimes discouraging when we can't recall accurately a verse we have worked hard to memorize. The truth is, however, *all* forms of discipline require work and are often discouraging. The one who perseveres in any discipline, despite the hard work and discouraging times, reaps the reward the discipline is meant to produce.

The Navigators have emphasized Scripture memorization for over sixty years. Their *Topical Memory System*, which teaches principles of memorization and provides sixty key verses of Scripture to memorize, is available from NavPress and may be purchased through your local Christian bookstore. If you have never developed the discipline of Scripture memorization, I highly recommend this program.

11

THE DISCIPLINE OF CHOICES

*Just as you used to offer the parts of your body
in slavery to impurity and to ever-increasing wickedness,
so now offer them in slavery to righteousness
leading to holiness.*

ROMANS 6:19

CENTRAL IDEA
Holiness of character is developed one choice at a time as
we choose to act righteously in every situation we
encounter during the day.

IDENTIFYING THE ISSUES
Excerpted and adapted from *The Discipline of Grace*, pages 181-200.

❝The Bible is a very relevant book, continually facing us
with a series of choices—for example, sinful attitudes and
actions to "put off" and Christlike character to "put on"
(Ephesians 5:25-32). Through repetitive choices we
develop Christlike habits of living.

Yet we do not make our choices in a vacuum. They are
determined by the convictions we have developed and the
conscious or unconscious commitments we have made.
Given the remaining presence of indwelling sin, we can
make the right choices only through dependence on the

enabling power of the Holy Spirit. But all of these principles and means of spiritual growth find their ultimate fulfillment only when we obey God's commandments one choice at a time.

The pursuit of holiness is like quilt-making. Each one-foot quilt square has a design sewn into it that determines the overall pattern of the quilt. Yet those individual squares, as beautiful as they are, do not make a quilt. Only when they are sewn together with a narrow strip of cloth between each row of squares do they become a quilt.

So also we have the quilt square of discipline, the square of dependence, of commitment, of convictions, and of beholding the glory of Christ in the gospel. Each of these "squares" is beautiful in itself. But if we just look at these means of holiness individually, we still do not have the "quilt" of holiness. What joins all these means together to form the "quilt of holiness" is obedience. And we obey one choice, or one stitch, at a time.

What happens when we make wrong choices, when we choose to sin instead of obey God's Word? We train ourselves in the wrong direction. We reinforce the sinful habits we have already developed and allow them to gain greater strength in our souls.

The message implied in 2 Peter 2:14, about false teachers who have *trained* themselves to become "experts in greed," is sobering. It is possible to discipline ourselves in the wrong direction. We usually think of disciplined people as those who "have their act together." Obviously, we are disciplining ourselves in one direction or the other by the choices we make. The question is, *In which direction are we disciplined?*

God wants us to train ourselves in the right direction by making the right choices. Frankly, this is where the going gets tough. We may make a commitment of sorts to put a particular sin out of our lives, but when the temptation to indulge that sin comes once again, we are unwilling to say no.

Only through making the right choices to obey God's

Word will we break the habits of sin and develop habits of holiness. Making the right choices to obey God rather than the desires of our sinful natures (or flesh) necessarily involves the discipline of *mortification* (or putting to death). From Romans 8:13 we see that to make the right choices it is necessary to mortify, or put to death, the misdeeds of the body. The misdeeds of the body are the sinful actions we commit in thought, word, or deed (Colossians 3:5). This is something *we* must do, not something we turn over to God.

Although mortification is our responsibility, it can be done only through God's enabling power—"*if by the Holy Spirit*" (Romans 8:13). This keeps our duty from being dismissed as only "a work of the flesh." Mortification attempted only by human willpower always ends in either self-righteousness (pride) or frustration (guilt).

Paul did not say to mortify indwelling sin, but rather *sins*, which are the various expressions of indwelling sin. We cannot eliminate indwelling sin in this life. Sin will be with us until the day we die. To mortify a sin means to *subdue* it or to *deprive it of its power*. The *goal* of mortification is *to weaken the habits of sin* so that we do make the right choices.

Mortification involves dealing with all known sin in one's life. Without a purpose to obey all of God's Word, isolated attempts to mortify a particular sin are of no avail. An attitude of *universal* obedience in every area of life is essential. There must also be a *constant* fight against it. We must put sin to death continually, every day, as the flesh seeks to assert itself in various ways in our lives. No believer, no matter how spiritually mature, ever gets beyond the need to mortify the sinful deeds of the body. To mortify sin we must focus on its true nature, that is, hate all sin for what it really is: an expression of rebellion against God, a breaking of His law, a despising of His authority, a grieving of His heart. And yet God in Christ died for those sins.

We must realize that in putting sin to death we are

saying no to our own desires. Sin most often appeals to us through our desires. Not all desires, of course, are sinful. Many desires are positive (to know God, to obey Him, and to serve Him).

Mortification involves a struggle between what we *know* to be right (our convictions) and what we *desire* to do (Galatians 5:17). It is always emotionally painful to say no to those desires, especially when they represent recurring sin patterns, because those desires run deep and strong. They cry out for fulfillment. That is why Paul used such strong language as "put to death."

That is also why we need the help of one or two friends to engage in the struggle with us. These friends should be believers who share our commitment to the pursuit of holiness, who will be mutually open with us about their own struggles, and who will not be scandalized by serious sins. We need at least one other person of like heart to pray with us, encourage us, and if necessary, admonish us. The principle underlying this aid to mortification is called *synergism* ("the sum of the parts, working together, is greater than each one working separately"), as in Ecclesiastes 4:9-10 ("two are better than one").

Remember the scissors illustration in session 5? Both the blade of "putting off" (mortification) and the blade of "putting on" (clothing ourselves with Christlike character) must be working together. Each must receive equal emphasis. The old Puritan preachers used to speak not only of *mortification* (putting sin to death) but also of *vivification* (bringing to life the traits of the new person in Christ). Both are "by the Spirit" (Galatians 5:16-23, Colossians 3:12-14). The indwelling Spirit instructs us, enables us, gifts us, and strengthens us in God's grace for this task (Philippians 4:13, 2 Timothy 2:1).

The discipline of mortification will be attended by a certain amount of failure; henceforth, as always, we stand before God on the basis of His grace rather than our performance. Once again, we straddle a fine line between using grace as an excuse for sin and using grace as a remedy for our sin.

The solution to staying on the right side of the fine line between using and abusing grace is repentance. The road to repentance is godly sorrow (2 Corinthians 7:10). Godly sorrow is developed when we focus on the true nature of sin as an offense against God rather than something that makes us feel guilty. Godly sorrow, in turn, leads us to repentance. Having come to repentance, however, we must by faith lay hold of the cleansing blood of Christ, which alone can cleanse our consciences.

Where will the desire to engage in the discipline of mortification come from? It will only come from the gratitude and joy of knowing that however miserably I have failed, God's grace is greater than my sin. Only the gospel will keep us living by grace. And only grace will give us the courage and motivation to mortify sin and to keep seeking to make the right choices even when we fail so often.99

DEVELOPING THE DISCIPLINE OF GRACE

1. The Bible is like life itself in presenting us with a constant series of choices, many with moral consequences. Consider, for openers, your daily commute to work each morning (or your daily drive somewhere else). What are some possible moral consequences of the following everyday choices?

✢ The thoughts I choose to think while driving.

✢ The way I choose to drive.

✢ Whether I choose to stop by the roadside to help a motorist in distress.

♣ The radio station or tapes I choose to listen to.

2. Read Ephesians 5:25-32 and list at least five moral
   "either–or" choices that believers are faced with.

3. One sinful choice usually leads to another, and eventually to a habit, because sin clouds our reason, dulls our
   conscience, stimulates our sinful desires, and weakens
   our will. Think of a sinful habit you have found hard to
   shake off. When you have chosen to give in to this, how
   have you experienced your reason being clouded, your
   conscience being dulled, your desire being stimulated,
   or your will to resist being weakened? Give an example
   of this happening to you.

4. a. Given the habit-forming nature of sin, what remedy
      does Paul propose in Romans 6:19?

   b. What does this look like in practice? For instance,
      how would it apply to the situation you described
      in question 3?

5. When exhorting Timothy, and us, to "exercise thyself
   rather unto godliness" (1 Timothy 4:7, KJV), Paul used a

word from the athletic arena that describes the physical exercise regimen of young men as they prepared themselves to compete in the Olympic games of that day. Just as those young men trained themselves physically in order to compete in the games, so also we are to train ourselves spiritually toward godliness. How do we "exercise ourselves" in the spiritual realm?

6. Think of one of the persistent sin patterns in your life that you have already identified and committed yourself to uproot in previous sessions. You need to be especially vigilant in this area to make the right choices. You have already made too many wrong choices; that is why this sin pattern is so deeply entrenched. No doubt you would like to be rid of this sin and have prayed to God to take it away. But are you willing to say *no* to it, to "put to death [mortify] the misdeeds of the body"? If so, record here the choice you will make the next time the temptation presents itself, and then look to the Holy Spirit to work in you "to will and to act" (Philippians 2:13) in carrying out that commitment. (You don't need to discuss your answer with your group.)

7. a. How do you feel when you think about having to make that choice?

b. What will help you make the right choice?

8. People vary in their ability to discipline themselves. The more naturally disciplined person wonders why everyone else can't be as successful in mortification as he or she is. But often all that person has done is exchanged one sin (impure thoughts, for example) for another (pride). Another person, less self-disciplined, tries to mortify some particular sin by sheer willpower, but fails and becomes frustrated. Which of the two errors—pride or frustration—do you most commonly fall into when you try to mortify sin on your own apart from utter dependence on the Spirit?

9. a. Think of an unusually persistent sin in your life. If we are to succeed in putting sin to death, we must realize that the sin we are dealing with is none other than a continual exalting of our desire over God's known will. This will also involve intense struggle. Since mortification is a difficult work, aimed at subduing strong desires and deeply ingrained habits, we need the help of one or two friends to engage in the struggle with us. Name one or two trusted people you can turn to:

b. If you can't think of anyone to trust with this issue, why do you suppose that's the case?

❑ My friends are untrustworthy.
❑ I'm too proud to admit this weakness.
❑ My friends are good people, but they would never be able to understand how someone like me could struggle with this.
❑ I don't have any close friends.
❑ I don't believe I need anyone else to help me with this.
❑ Other:

108

c. If you don't believe you know even one person who can struggle with you in this area, what can you do about this problem?

10. a. How does each of these passages describe the job of helping our friends struggle against sin?

Galatians 6:1-2

1 Thessalonians 5:11

Hebrews 3:13

Hebrews 10:24-25

James 5:16

b. Do these passages motivate you to seek help from your friends in your battle against sin? Why, or why not?

11. At the end of your group discussion, pray for one another in your battle against sin. You might divide into pairs and pray for your partners.

WHAT'S THE POINT OF ALL THIS?

All that we have studied in the last few sessions has been leading us to this point. We do not become more holy either by discipline or by dependence. Neither do we become more holy by committing ourselves to God or by developing Bible-based convictions. We become more holy by obedience to the Word of God, by choosing to obey His will as revealed in the Scriptures in all the various circumstances of our lives.

Next we focus on the discipline of watching. Meditate on Matthew 26:41 and read chapter 12 of *The Discipline of Grace* in preparation for the next session.

12

The Discipline
of Watching

"Watch and pray so that you will not fall into temptation.
The spirit is willing, but the body is weak."
MATTHEW 26:41

CENTRAL IDEA

With the world, Satan, and the flesh arrayed against us, we must watch against the temptations that constantly beset us. We can effectively do so by knowing our enemy, knowing our weaknesses and strengths, and mounting a good offense, that is, by meditating on God's Word and by prayer.

IDENTIFYING THE ISSUES

Excerpted and adapted from *The Discipline of Grace*, pages 201-216.

"A lack of watchfulness contributed to the world's greatest maritime disaster, the collision of the steamship *Titanic* with an iceberg, a mere two days from completing its maiden transatlantic voyage. Radio messages from other ships warning of ice were either taken lightly or ignored altogether. Neither did the crew bother with binoculars for the lookout in the crow's nest. Despite the fact that the captain knew they were sailing directly into an area of dangerous ice packs, he had the engines going at full speed.

In hindsight, such an indifferent attitude toward the single most dangerous hazard to North Atlantic shipping seems to be the height of irresponsibility. Yet this is the same attitude with which many believers approach the Christian life. Every day we sail through a sea infested with icebergs of temptation. Yet our cavalier ("it couldn't happen to me") attitude toward sin contributes to the downfall of self-confident Christians.

If we are going to watch against temptation, we need intelligence information about the enemy. The Bible speaks of three sources of temptation: the world, the flesh, and the Devil (Ephesians 2:1-3; 1 John 2:15-17, 4:3-5). The "world," or the sinful society in which we live, subtly pressures us to conform to its values and practices. It creeps up on us, pervasively and relentlessly, little by little. What was once unthinkable becomes thinkable, then doable, and finally acceptable to society at large. Sin becomes respectable, so Christians finally embrace it. I believe Christians are no more than five to ten years behind the world in embracing most sinful practices.

The Devil is the god of this world and the ultimate strategist behind all the temptations that come to us from society. It is difficult and perhaps unnecessary to try to distinguish between a temptation from the world and one from Satan. In general, however, temptations from the world tend to be subtle and gradual, whereas Satan's direct attacks are more often sudden and violent—like that of a lion (1 Peter 5:8).

As dangerous as are the world and the Devil, neither is our greatest problem. Our greatest source of temptation dwells within us. What the Apostle Paul called the flesh, or the sinful nature, is the principle of sin that remains within us, even though it no longer exercises dominion. Indwelling sin now wages guerrilla warfare against us—a most difficult warfare to defend against, for it is so insidious (Romans 7:21-25).

As a Pogo cartoon years ago expressed it, "We have met the enemy and it is us." Our flesh is always searching out opportunities, like a radar antenna, to gratify itself according to the particular sinful desires each of us has. Our scanner will pick up some temptations that arise from our temperament: anger, or moroseness, or laziness, or a tendency to control others. We may be exposed to other temptations because of the occupation or profession we are in. The advertising copywriter may be under pressure to "puff" a product. The salesperson may be asked to lie. The person who has a company expense account may be tempted to cheat, and so may students in a competitive academic environment.

We can never get to the place where we don't need to watch, even in areas where we think we are strong, lest we fall due to our self-confidence. Without knowledge of ourselves and our own particular weaknesses toward sin, we cannot watch against those temptations. Realize that your "temptation antenna" constantly scans your world looking for those areas of sin. Then watch and pray against them.

I have often heard a well-known Christian teacher say, "There is no sin which I am not capable of committing." Such humility is our only safeguard, as we must realize how powerful indwelling sin still is. And we need to watch in areas where we think we are strong, because that is where we are apt to trust ourselves and not depend on God.

Another area where we need to be watchful is the little things of everyday life—the little lie, the little bit of pride, the little lustful glance, or the little bit of gossip. These may seem too small to bother about, but life is largely a mosaic of little events and little deeds. It is the decision we make when the cashier at the supermarket gives us too much change, or the waiter at the restaurant understates our bill, that reveals whether we are honest or not.

You may think I trivialize life by frequently using illustrations of sins that some consider "no big deal," but the minutiae of life are where most of us live day after day. We seldom have to say *no* to an outright temptation to adultery. We often have to say *no* to the temptation to the lustful look or thought. And as someone has said, "He that despises little things shall fall little by little."

Turning Christian liberty into a license to sin is an evil that is ingrained in sinful human nature. We easily construe liberty as the right to do whatever we want. Knowing that our sinful human nature has this tendency, we ought to be especially watchful against it. In my younger years the Christian community attempted to do this watching for us by drafting various lists of "don'ts." This practice resulted in a modern Pharisaism wherein specific rules of behavior, or "sins" to avoid, were added to the Bible as God's will for us.

More recently we have reacted against such legalism, perhaps rightly so. But we need to be watchful that in asserting our freedom to drive close to the edge, we do not give the flesh an opportunity to lead us over the precipice into sin.

How can we effectively watch against the temptations that constantly beset us? The old adage "The best defense is a good offense" is good advice for watching against temptation. The best offense for avoiding evil is meditation on the Word of God (Psalm 1:2, 119:11) and prayer (1 Thessalonians 5:17,22). These are the only two spiritual exercises we are encouraged to do continually. Remember that Jesus told us to watch *and* pray (Matthew 26:41). We are not capable of watching by ourselves; we need the Lord (Psalm 127:1, Matthew 6:13).

Furthermore, the gospel of God's forgiveness of our sins through Christ's death frees us to face those sins honestly and bring them to the cross and Jesus' cleansing blood. The freedom and joy that then come from a cleansed conscience create the desire and give us the right motive to deal with those sins. We cannot effectively pursue holiness without going back again and again to the

114

gospel.**99**

DEVELOPING THE DISCIPLINE OF GRACE

1. The indifference of the *Titantic's* captain and crew toward the hazards for North Atlantic shippers resulted in the world's greatest maritime disaster. This irresponsibility resembles the cavalier attitude many believers have toward icebergs of temptation.

   a. When has someone you love hit upon an "iceberg" (such as marital failure, financial bankruptcy, drug addiction, or a job loss due to ethical violation) that tore a hole in his or her ship?

   b. What were the signs this person failed to watch for?

   c. As you think about this person's sin, do you tend to think, "I would never do something like that"? Explain.

2. a. What are some sins you can't imagine ever committing?

   b. How do you respond to the warning that you should consider yourself capable of even these things? (Are you skeptical? Sobered? Why?)

3. a. Read Matthew 26:36-56. What temptations do you think Jesus faced in this situation?

   b. How did watching and praying help Him resist those temptations?

   c. Instead of watching and praying with Jesus, His disciples fell asleep. What temptations overtook them because they were too weak to resist?

   d. In verse 41, Jesus said they would have been strong enough to resist those temptations if they had simply disciplined themselves to watch and pray. Why do you suppose watching and praying would have made any difference?

4. "The world" pressures us to conform to its values and practices through advertising, pop psychology, magazines, movies, and television programs. Give an example of how you have experienced this pressure.

5. Do you agree that "Christians are no more than five to ten years behind the world in embracing most sinful practices"? Why, or why not?

6. While it is difficult to distinguish between an attack from Satan and a temptation from the world, sometimes it does seem that Satan is attacking us directly. For instance, a Sunday school teacher was sitting alone in church one Sunday because his wife was ill. A woman from his class, who apparently had an unhappy marriage, sat down next to him and subtly began to suggest an affair. This temptation came out of nowhere without warning, in an environment where one would least expect it. This would appear to be a direct frontal assault from the Devil, whereas temptation from the world comes over time through little indiscretions. The sex act is then fantasized in the mind before it is eventually acted out.

Can you recall any experiences when a temptation to sin seemed to assault you out of nowhere? If so, describe it.

7. The world and the Devil act in concert with an evil desire within us, which constantly searches for occasions to express itself. It is like a radar system constantly scanning the environment for temptations to which it can respond. For instance, Jerry Bridges' radar used to identify ice cream stores without fail.

What does your "temptation radar" scan for? (Or what does your car seem to brake for, almost invariably?) Try to be honest with yourself in your answer, even if you don't feel comfortable sharing your entire answer with your group.

❏ Donut shops
❏ Garage sales

❑ New model cars (or grand old dames)
❑ Cute members of the opposite sex
❑ Scandalous or gossipy news
❑ Magazines in checkout lines
❑ Skin flicks on cable TV in hotel rooms
❑ Other (name it):

8. Since each of us is vulnerable in different areas, it's important to identify them and then be honest with ourselves about our own weak spots. For example, knowing his own lustful heart, Bridges has made a personal commitment not to turn on the television at random when he is alone in a hotel room. Think of one of your own weaknesses. What would be a wise precaution you should take to guard yourself in this vulnerable area?

9. Give an example of a temptation you face because of your environment or occupation.

10. Bridges prays, "Lord, keep me on a short leash." That is, "Don't let me get away with the little sins. Give me a tender conscience that will recognize the little sins and sound the alarm bell in my heart." Would you be willing to commit to praying this daily for yourself? Why, or why not?

WHAT'S THE POINT OF ALL THIS?

In previous sessions we addressed the area of persistent sin patterns in our lives, those temptations to which we are especially vulnerable. We have seen that, having identified our own areas of vulnerability, we should make definite commitments regarding them, pray about them, and memorize specific verses of Scripture that will strengthen us against those temptations. Now we should add another help: Be especially watchful against them.

Next time we focus on the discipline of adversity. Meditate on Hebrews 12:7 and read chapter 13 of *The Discipline of Grace* in preparation for the next session.

13

THE DISCIPLINE
OF ADVERSITY

Endure hardship as discipline; God is treating you as sons.
For what son is not disciplined by his father?
HEBREWS 12:7

CENTRAL IDEA

God gives us the discipline of adversity as a means of our sanctification. Our role in this discipline is to respond to it and to acquiesce to whatever God may be doing, even though a particular instance of adversity makes no sense to us. As we do this we will see in due time the fruit of the Spirit produced in our lives.

IDENTIFYING THE ISSUES

Excerpted and adapted from *The Discipline of Grace*, pages 217-231.

66Adversity is not a discipline we undertake ourselves, but it is imposed on us by God as a means of spiritual growth, "that we may share in his holiness" (Hebrews 12:10). Here again, as in chapter 5, the word *discipline* refers to a means of *God's* spiritual child-training. (In other chapters *discipline* indicates the spiritual training for which we ourselves are responsible.)

120

The Lord disciplines those He loves (Proverbs 3:11-12, Hebrews 12:6). Discipline is not the mark of a harsh father, but rather of a father who is deeply concerned for the welfare and maturity of his children.

It is wrong to make light of, or despise, the Lord's discipline (Hebrews 12:5). We discount His discipline when we view it only as something to be endured and be relieved of, rather than as something for our profit. We also despise God's discipline of adversity when we fail to see God's hand in it, but instead view adversities as chance occurrences, without a guiding purpose (Ecclesiastes 7:13-14, Isaiah 45:7, Lamentations 3:37-38, Amos 3:6).

The other improper response is to "lose heart when he rebukes you" (Hebrews 12:5). How disheartening to think God disciplines us out of anger; how encouraging to know He does so out of love. Though our feelings may tell us otherwise, this is the abundant testimony of Scripture.

Punishment serves either to execute justice or correct character flaws. A good parent punishes a child for the latter reason. Although today we usually equate discipline with punishment, the biblical use of the word *discipline*, as we have seen, has a broader meaning. Punishment is but one aspect of the overall program of God's spiritual child-training. All of God's discipline, including punishment for disobedience that He sends to us in the form of adversity, is administered in love and for our welfare.

Regrettably, human parents do not always administer punishment in love and for the child's welfare. When a parent inflicts punishment out of sinful passions, neither justice nor correction is in view. God obviously does not have sinful passion, so we must never equate His punishment of us with the emotions or motives we so often see in a human parent.

God does punish in the execution of justice (Romans 12:19, 2 Thessalonians 1:6). But as far as believers are concerned, God has already executed on His Son the justice we should have received. Christ fully satisfied the justice of God and turned away His wrath from us. Therefore,

God's punishment of us is always corrective, always administered in love, and always for our welfare. Yet Satan will twist this message, especially in times of adversity, so gird yourself daily with the gospel (see Ephesians 6:13-17). All hardship of whatever kind has a disciplinary purpose for us. This does not necessarily mean a particular hardship is related to a specific act or habit of sin in our lives, but that every expression of discipline has a purpose in a believer's life—to conform us to the likeness of Christ.

Part of the sanctifying process of adversity is its mystery, that is, our inability to make any sense out of a particular hardship. His ways, being infinitely higher than our ways, will usually remain a mystery to us (Romans 11:33). Despite our pain and perplexity, we are reassured: "God is treating you as sons" (Hebrews 12:7). Remember, God knows exactly what and how much adversity will develop more Christlikeness in us and He will not bring, or allow to come into our lives, any more than is needful for His purpose. Christlike character, or fruit of the Spirit, is developed only in the crucible of real-life experience.

In order to profit most from the discipline of hardship, we need to submit to it (Hebrews 12:9-10). If we respected our fathers' discipline, how much more should we submit to God's discipline. Our fathers' discipline was at best imperfect, both in motive and in application. But God's discipline is perfect, exactly suited to our needs.

How then do we submit to God's discipline? Negatively, it means we do not become angry at God, or charge Him with injustice, when very difficult circumstances come into our lives. Positively, we submit to God's discipline when we accept all hardship as coming from His loving hand for our good (1 Peter 5:6). We should submit to and trust in God's providential dealings with us, knowing that there is still much in our characters that needs improving.

Submitting to God's discipline doesn't mean we should not pray for relief from the difficulty or should not seek legitimate means to gain relief, as long as we are still submissive to Him regarding the outcome. Jesus' prayer in Gethsemane the night before His crucifixion is the supreme example of this: "Yet not as I will, but as you will" (Matthew 26:39).

Anyone who has tried to rear children in a godly manner will debate what is the appropriate manner or degree of discipline for a child. God, however, *knows* what is best for each one of us. He doesn't have to debate with Himself over what is most suitable for us. He never brings more pain than is needed to accomplish His purpose—which is conforming us to the likeness of Christ, or sharing in God's holiness. That is the highest good to which the believer can aspire.

All afflictions are painful (Hebrews 12:11). We should be honest and admit the pain. Later on, however, the discipline produces a "harvest of righteousness and peace" (12:12). The road to holiness is paved with adversity. If you want to be holy, expect the discipline of God through the heartaches and disappointments He brings or allows to come into our lives.

This harvest of "peace" may be what comes with maturity in this life or the rest that comes ultimately to the believer in eternity. Both concepts are taught in Scripture. Concerning this life, our sufferings produce faith which produces perseverance which, in turn, produces mature and holy character (Romans 5:3-4, James 1:2-5).

Our ultimate hope, though, is not in maturity of character in this life, as valuable as that is, but in the *perfection* of character in eternity. The often-painful process of being transformed into His likeness will be over. We shall be completely conformed to the likeness of the Lord Jesus Christ.

Visualize a pair of old-fashioned balance scales. On one side are all your sufferings, all your heartaches and disappointments, all your adversities of whatever kind from whatever source. Of course, the scales tip way to that side. But then picture on the other side all the glory that will be revealed in us. Can you see how completely the scales now bottom out on that second side?

Paul said our sufferings *are not worth comparing* with

123

the glory we will experience in eternity. This is not to say that our present hardships are not painful. Nothing said in this chapter is intended to minimize the pain and perplexity of adversity. But Scripture reassures us that the God who disciplines us will also glorify us.

Learning to live by grace instead of by performance helps us to accept the discipline of adversity. For one thing, we realize that God is not disciplining us because of our bad performance but, on the contrary, because of His love for us. We also learn to accept that whatever our situation is, it is far better than we deserve. None of us wants to receive from God what we actually deserve, for that would be only eternal punishment. So we learn not to ask, "Why did this happen to me?" (meaning, what did I do to deserve such bad treatment from God?). And we learn, as the Apostle Paul did with his thorn in the flesh, that God's grace is sufficient for us (2 Corinthians 12:9). **99**

DEVELOPING THE DISCIPLINE OF GRACE

1. Hebrews 12:4-13 illustrates how God uses adversity to discipline us in godliness. Read that passage. In which of the following ways do you typically respond to painful circumstances? (Check as many as apply.)

❏ I often despise God's discipline by viewing adversity as something to be escaped as quickly as possible.

❏ I often lose heart, feeling that God is mad at me and must not love me very much when He allows me to suffer.

❏ I often get angry, asking, "Why did this happen to me?" and accusing God of injustice. However, after an initial outburst, I get over my rage.

❏ My anger at God may continue for months, even years.

❏ I often accept hardship as coming from God's hand for my good, even when the situation makes no sense to me.

❑ I openly rebel against Him, thinking I know better what's good for me.

❑ My primary response is one of humble submission and trust.

❑ I diligently apply God's mind and will to my situation, trying to figure it out.

❑ I renounce my self-will and resign myself to God's will—not always immediately, but usually in due time.

❑ I throw a "pity party" and invite as many friends as I can to behold what manner of suffering I endure.

❑ I pray for relief from the difficulty and seek legitimate means to gain that relief.

❑ Other (describe your response):

2. We cannot know for certain if a particular adversity is related to some specific sin in our lives. But the Holy Spirit will catch our attention if we need to know in order to deal with a particular sin. If no linkage comes to mind, we can pray, asking God what He wants us to consciously learn.

   Prayerfully reflect over your life. Can you cite one situation when the connection between a painful hardship and God's loving disciplinary purpose was clear to you? What was God's aim in that situation?

3. The writer of Hebrews presumes a rational, ideal family model—one where the children respect the father who disciplines them (because he does so for the right reasons), and thus they will submit to that discipline (12:9-10). The biblical writer draws a parallel between our imperfect human fathers and our perfect heavenly Father. Some readers struggle with this passage because their own fathers were so different from the heavenly ideal. What was your own earthly father's style of discipline?

❑ I could see the loving, character-developing pur-
pose behind my father's discipline of me.
❑ My dad abused me with his anger.
❑ My dad never disciplined me.
❑ My dad did what he thought was best, but he was
often wrong.
❑ I had no father during most or all of my childhood.
❑ Other (describe your father's discipline):

4. How do you think your father's way of disciplining
you affects the way you respond to God's discipline?

5. The road to holiness is paved with adversity but eventually leads to a "harvest of righteousness and peace"
(Hebrews 12:12). Where are you along that road? (What
kind of harvest have you seen?)

6. a. Are you experiencing a painful situation right now?
If so, describe it.

   b. How do you intend to handle this situation in light
   of what you know about discipline?

7. Remember the airplane metaphor—with the two
wings, dependence and discipline? We have now cov-
ered six duties of discipleship, or things we can and
must do to grow in godliness. Those six constitute the
wing of discipline. But counterbalancing that is the

weighty wing on the left—dependence on God—without which no growth is possible. On that wing we find two ways in which God disciplines us. These eight factors are the means by which we become like Christ.

How would you describe in your own words the six ways we discipline ourselves and the two ways in which God disciplines us?

The wing of discipline—
six ways we discipline ourselves:

✤ Beholding Christ in the gospel

✤ Making a commitment to holiness

✤ Developing Bible-based convictions

✤ Acting on choices

✤ Mortifying sin

✤ Watching and praying against temptation

The wing of dependence—
two ways God disciplines us:

✤ By adversity

✤ By grace

It is crucial to relate our response to adversity and all our self-discipline back to God's grace, lest we come to think we are in a performance relationship with Him. Performing these disciplines does not earn us one iota of favor with God. His favor comes to us strictly through the merit of Jesus Christ. We practice these disciplines, not to earn favor with God, but because they are the means God has given to enable us to pursue holiness.

In the course of this study, we have seen that grace and discipline—both God's discipline of us and our discipline of ourselves—far from being opposed to each other, are inextricably united together in God's program of sanctification. God's discipline *is* based on grace, there is no question about that.

8. You made some commitments back in session 9. What habits do you plan to begin or continue as a result of this study? What steps will you take to act on these commitments?

9. Express your dependence on God through a protracted time of prayer. Include some time to praise God for the grace He has given you through Christ.

❖ ❖ ❖

Remember, "discipleship without desire is drudgery." Training in godliness, with desire instilled by the gospel, is anything but drudgery.